Parsonally Speaking

ROY BOLITHO

Minstrel
Eastbourne

First published 1991

Cover illustration and text cartoons by Taffy Davies

British Library Cataloguing in Publication Data

Bolitho, Roy
  Parsonally speaking
  1. English wit and humour
  I. Title
  828'.91402'080922

ISBN 1–85424–146–X

Printed in Great Britain for
Minstrel, an imprint of Monarch Publications Ltd
1 St Anne's Road, Eastbourne, E Sussex BN21 3UN by
Clays Ltd, St. Ives plc
Typeset by J&L Composition Ltd, Filey, North Yorkshire

CONTENTS

INTRODUCTION

This collection of anecdotes, which comes with my blessing, represents the funny side of religion. And humour certainly seems to be increasing in church circles.

You may feel a stab of envy when you read the wit of others. You may already know some of the anecdotes. But I am sure that this anthology will amuse and entertain you.

So, sit back, hang up your dog collar, and enjoy some laughs from the world of the church!

SERVICE WITH A SMILE

You don't normally expect chuckles at a wedding service. Sometimes, though, they do happen ...

From Lima, Peru, this extraordinary incident that quite flabbergasted the minister who was officiating at a wedding.

Looking radiant in her white gown, Teresa Romero Garcia was about to be wed to Alcides Zelada Saldan when there came an interruption.

Down the aisle charged Saldan's legal wife—with his five children right behind.

'Stop!' cried the legal wife. 'That's *my* husband there.'

'Daddy, Daddy!' shouted the five children.

Shaldan didn't know where to look. Teresa fainted. Then the 'bridegroom' fled.

'He left home this morning,' wept Señora Saldan, 'and said he was going to work.'

'I'm afraid,' the minister said solemnly, 'we have had a very short-term bride here today.'

11

Smile, please, at the Cornish parson who did not come out very well in a photograph. His mouth was open, his eyes were squinting, and his expression was rather grim.

At the next wedding, he was advised to say 'Cheese' for the photographer.

'Cheese?' the clergyman said, looking surprised. 'I thought the word you had to say was Mouse.'

A vicar in Dorset reports that he once held out his prayer book for the best man to put the ring on. Instead, the confused young man slapped his hand on the book, almost knocking it out of the clergyman's hand.

'No,' explained the vicar quietly. 'You don't have to say, "I swear to tell the truth, the whole truth and nothing but the truth."'

On another occasion, the same vicar told a couple to kneel down while he said the blessing at the chancel steps. Then, after pronouncing them man and wife, he whispered: 'Now follow me to the altar.'

But as the couple started to shuffle along on their knees, the vicar said: 'You may walk on your feet, you know.'

An American minister tells the story of a man who came into the church before a wedding.

'Is someone called Paterson getting married here in a minute?'

That is correct,' nodded the minister.

'Well,' the man said, 'that guy's a swindler, and I have a warrant for his arrest. But I'll sit down and wait until the ceremony is over.'

'Very well,' said the minister. 'Friends of the groom, second aisle on the right.'

A Birmingham clergyman tells this story:

'An invitation was sent to this young man to say that his best friend was getting married. Well, the man duly turned up in church, only to be greeted by his girlfriend, who bashfully handed him a wedding ring.

"You'll be needing this," said the girl. And so, the man who had arrived as a guest, found himself exchanging vows and being married to the girl, Rosemary. I must say, he looked pretty stunned, but he didn't object and, as far as I know, they are still happily married.'

There were titters in church in Scottsville, Michigan, USA, when the Revd Snow officiated at the marriage of Miss Christmas and Mr Noel.

13

ACE RETORTERS

Here are some memorable examples of the spontaneous rejoinder, made by clergymen. This type of repartee apparently dates back to the Restoration period of the 17th century when the witty, incisive reply became socially acceptable.

The late Pope John XXIII was once asked how many people worked in the Vatican.

'About half of them,' he smiled.

At an ecclesiastical gathering in the north of England, a clergyman who spent much of his time trying to evangelise factory workers was questioned about his work by one of his superiors.

'I am taking God into industry,' the clergyman said proudly.

'How interesting for him,' came the reply. 'And where are you planning to take him next?'

In Nottingham, a man was walking his dog back home late one night. Passing the vicarage, he was surprised to see the vicar down on his knees tinkering with his old car.

'Saying your prayers at this late hour, vicar?' joked the man.

'No,' came the swift reply, 'I'm just giving the car a midnight service.'

A garage mechanic in Cornwall brought the vicar's car back after repairs and wanted to know if everything was all right.

'Young man,' said the vicar, 'you appear to have left undone those things you ought to have done.'

'On Friday I shall be fifty,' said the vicar to the curate.

Puzzled, the curate said, 'But didn't you say that last year?'

'Well, I am not one of these people who say one thing today and something else tomorrow.'

After being told about a school for soothsayers, a parson quipped: 'No doubt, it was a prophet-making concern.'

Budding young author to his vicar: 'Everybody in this town has a book in him, you know, vicar.'

Vicar: 'What a good place for it.'

A Devon man had a reputation for being a real bore when talking about his fishing trips.

After one day by the river, he met the local vicar on his way home and explained, not for the first time, about the one that got away.

'Do you know,' the fellow cried, 'it was *that* long!' And he indicated a space from here to there. 'Vicar, I never saw such a fish.'

The vicar said quietly, 'That I believe.'

A new vicar was doing the rounds in a Cornish village, meeting his parishioners. At one house, a voice from inside answered his knock with: 'Ooh, is that you, angel?'

'No,' the vicar called, 'but I'm from the same department.'

After delivering a sermon, a conceited young clergyman asked his bishop's opinion of it.

19

'I think your sermon resembled the great sword of Charlemagne,' the bishop said.

'It was a victorious sword, was it not?' said the clergyman, pleased with himself.

'Indeed it was,' the bishop retorted. 'And it was also long and flat.'

At the outbreak of World War Two, an anxious lady said to her vicar: 'I think God will be on our side, don't you?'

'I am more concerned that we should be on God's side,' the vicar replied.

A medieval riddle, attributed to a cleric named Bar-Hebraeus, leader of the Christian community in Syria in the 13th century, went like this:

'When a cock wakes in the morning, why does he hold one foot in the air?'

'I don't know. When a cock wakes in the morning, why *does* he hold one foot in the air?'

'Because if he lifted both he would fall down.'

At a party, one American guest was boring everyone with his experiences in the marines during the war.

'Do you know,' he droned, 'I was torpedoed in the Pacific and lived for a week on a can of sardines.'

'Really!' exclaimed the vicar, one of the many reluctant listeners. 'Weren't you afraid of falling off?'

A man said to the rabbi: 'Please advise me. Every year my wife brings forth another baby. I have ten already and hardly enough money to pay for food. Rabbi, what can I do?'

'Do nothing,' came the reply.

Phone conversation.

Woman: 'My husband told me to tell you he's not in.'

Vicar: 'Good. Kindly tell him I'm glad I didn't call.'

In the 18th century in Poland, a man tugged at his rabbi's sleeve, crying: 'Rabbi, there are notorious thieves in our congregation!'

'That could be good,' the rabbi said. 'Since the

gates of mercy are so locked against us at this time, we might need their expertise to break the lock.'

A clergyman was listening to a young man telling a story that seemed endless.

'Well,' the fellow said at one point, 'to cut a long story short ...'

'Too late,' exclaimed the cleric.

'Happiness,' declared one parson, 'is the pursuit of something rather than the catching of it.'

The other parson commented: 'Sounds like racing for the final bus on a rainy night.'

A minister came out of church to find he had been 'booked' for a parking offence. In court, he waited until at last his name was called. The judge asked: 'Have you anything to say?'

'Yes,' the minister replied. 'Blessed are the merciful for they shall obtain mercy.'

After a fellow guest made some objectionable remarks at a dinner-dance, a vicar pointed this out to the host.

'Oh, he doesn't mean to be unpleasant,' the host said. 'He just says these things tongue-in-cheek.'

The vicar retorted: 'I think he confuses tongue-in-cheek with foot-in-mouth.'

Lord Ramsey, former Archbishop of Canterbury, was once asked if he ever looked up to the galleries of the House of Lords to see if there was anybody listening to him.

'I am *always* looking upwards to see if anybody is there,' Lord Ramsey replied.

When told that Lord Brougham, a lawyer with a somewhat unsavoury reputation, was arriving for a performance of *The Messiah*, Sydney Smith, sometime Canon of St Paul's Cathedral, snapped: 'Here comes counsel for the other side.'

A portly archbishop checked in at Glasgow airport, and he was deep in thought when the official handling his luggage said, 'You are slightly over-weight.'

'I know,' the archbishop replied, studying his ticket, 'but it isn't noticeable when I'm robed.'

SIGN LANGUAGE

More and more clergymen these days are displaying their sense of humour in the form of posters and notices, which they put up in or outside their church. Many of these are so well written you would think they had been created by professional gag-men.

Sign in a Rochdale church: 'God has a wonderful sense of humour. If you want to give him a laugh, tell him *your* plans for your life.'

On a church noticeboard in North London: 'Contact lens found in church. See vicar—if you can.'

Notice in a Brighton church: 'Plan ahead—it wasn't raining when Noah built the ark.'

Sign outside a church in Oxfordshire: 'It has been said that this church is full of hypocrites. Wrong—we can always find room for one more.'

Poster outside a church in Glasgow: 'The Carpenter requires joiners—apply within.'

In the porch of a chapel in West Cornwall: 'The congregation are reminded that the box in the porch marked "For the Sick" is for monetary contributions only.'

On the noticeboard of a church in Liverpool: 'The healthiest way to gamble is with a spade and a packet of garden seeds.'

Sign on a church door in Southampton: 'WET PAINT—watch it or wear it.'

A notice outside an Essex church proclaims: 'The Lord made heaven and earth, the sea and all that in them is, in six days—and he was self-employed.'

Sign on a garage door next to a church in South Kensington: 'No parking. Trespassers will be prayed for.'

Notice in a church porch in Barnsley, Yorkshire: 'There will be a prayer meeting on Friday 7.30 pm, to be followed by coffee and sandwiches. Come to pray, and stay to scoff.'

Prominent sign outside a church in California: 'Last chance to pray before the freeway.'

Spotted on a church noticeboard in Bristol: 'A smile is a curve which can set a lot of things straight.'

Sign outside a South London church: 'Come in and have your faith lifted.'

After his cleaner had been, a North Devon vicar put a notice on the newly-washed floor, saying: 'PLEASE DO NOT WALK ON THE WATER'.

Inviting parishioners to a communal celebration of penance, a Bristol vicar pinned a notice to the church noticeboard reading: 'If you don't have any sins, bring a friend who does!'

A sign outside a church in Beckenham, Kent, read: 'Prayer—the only commodity that isn't going up.'

Sign outside a North London church: 'Wanted—workers for God. Plenty of overtime.'

Outside a Baptist church: 'Church parkers only. Offenders will be baptised.'

A misprint on a chapel noticeboard: 'Sermon Sunday, February 6th: Change your Wife Through Prayer.'

Notice stuck on a church door: 'Sunday: The Revd M Farnsworth will talk on "Eternity and You". Come early—if you want to be sure of getting a seat at the back.'

Sign in a crematorium: 'All men are cremated equal.'

Notice outside a church hall where a film show was being held: 'You'll laugh, you'll cry, you'll kiss a pound goodbye.'

On a church noticeboard in a small Gloucestershire village: 'Despite inflation, the wages of sin remain the same.'

Sign in a church garden: 'Weeds are nature's rebellion against the gardener's dominion.'

Notice in a Birmingham car park: 'Unauthorised vehicles will be spirited away.'

Written on a board outside a Hampshire church: 'We have no connection with the Post Office. Just two collections every Sunday.'

Seen on the notice board of a church in Lancashire: 'For the Sunday morning service both the north and the south ends of the church will be used. Children will be baptised at both ends.'

CRANKY CLERICS

Eccentrics have sparkled in ecclesiastical circles over the years. I mention just a few who have amused and astonished us with their outrageous ideas and colourful ways.

A preacher, who came from an old Puritan family and lived in New Jersey in the mid-1800s, was obsessed by outer space. He would spend all night gazing at the moon and stars through a telescope.

He even persuaded the editor of his local paper to publish a piece stating that he had seen 'moon men' quite clearly. They were like human beings, he said, but only about four feet tall and covered with short copper-coloured hair. He insisted he kept seeing them standing around talking.

The preacher had a knack of making people believe what he believed. On his deathbed he was still muttering about his moon men.

The Revd R S Hawker, a 19th century vicar of Morwenstow, Cornwall, and a man of great vigour and humour, used to go to church with his ten pet cats.

Until one of them caught a mouse on a Sunday morning and ate it. Hawker excommunicated it.

When a small dog sat with him on the altar step, the vicar was asked why he didn't get rid of it. 'All creatures, clean and unclean, should find refuge here.'

Hawker was none too clean himself. A fussy young curate once piled up rubbish the vicar had left in the church. Taking it to Hawker's house, the curate said unctuously, 'This is all the rubbish I have collected in your church!'

The vicar of Morwenstow looked down on the curate from his great height. 'Kindly complete the pile,' he said, 'by seating yourself on top. Then we'll see the whole lot is quickly got rid of.'

Hawker loved riding bareback on a pony, accompanied by a black pig called Gyp which he would wash and brush until the animal shone.

Some days he could be seen riding the lanes on the back of a mule. 'The most fitting beast for a churchman,' he'd explain.

Some of Hawker's jokes have become legendary. One moonlit night, he rowed out to a rock dressed as a mermaid, with seaweed plaited into a wig and his legs covered in oilskin. He sat there using a hand mirror to flash moonbeams, and sang in a high-pitched voice.

He put on this performance for several nights, to the fascination of locals. He finished his act by singing 'God Save the King' and diving into the waves.

Robert Stephen Hawker wore his clothes until they were threadbare. His yellow garment made him look like a Tibetan lama.

He told his parishioners that it was the exact copy of one of the robes worn by ancient saints, who had an affinity with the East. But Hawker had bought it in Bideford. It was a blanket—an ordinary blanket—which he had made into a poncho by cutting a hole for the head!

In church, the Revd Hawker wore scarlet gloves, and, when baptising a baby, he would raise it in his arms, march up and down in his flowing purple cape, and boom: 'We receive this child into the congregation of Christ's flock!'

It was all very impressive and dramatic, and Hawker's baptisms became as popular as the local shows.

When he conducted a wedding ceremony, Hawker always took the ring and tossed it in the air for either the bridegroom or himself to catch it!

William Stonesmore, former Rector of Catthorpe, Lincolnshire, amused his flock by collecting odd items. When he died, his collection included: 130 wheelbarrows, 80 ploughs, 80 waggons, 200 pick-axes, 74 ladders, 400 pairs of shoes and 200 walking sticks.

A preacher in Georgia, USA, vowed some time ago that he would eat his hat if man ever landed on the moon and returned safely to earth.

Of course it happened—and people turned out from miles around to watch the man of cloth keep his word.

It took hours, but he managed to eat all of his old straw boater!

An Australian clergyman, Jim James, started to collect newspapers at an early age. He ended up with a lorry full of them and took the lot to some open ground. There, he meticulously rolled each newspaper up and erected for himself a small house consisting of nothing but newspapers, where he sometimes slept.

An eccentric preacher in Minnesota, USA, during the last century, actually lived in a large butter tub.

Another American preacher habitually went to bed in winter with his hot water bottle filled with hot tea.

There once was a vicar who enjoyed pulling people's legs. At a baptism, he would roll up his sleeves, dip his hands in the font and smile reassuringly at all present, saying, 'He should be in there *somewhere*.'

An 18th century vicar in Gloucestershire loved putting on lavish dinners ... for the dogs in the parish!

The Revd Andrew Taggart, vicar of Babbacombe church, and chaplain to Torquay United football club, has no doubts: 'Churches need a bit of fun!' he whoops.

And to offset any possible boredom in his church, he introduced a raffle based on hymn numbers.

He gives tickets to his 35-strong congregation and, if their number coincides with any of the hymn numbers sung during the service, they get a prize.

And when it comes to his sermon, if Revd Taggart spots anyone dozing he shouts their name out!

Cardinal Richelieu liked to jump up and down on furniture before interviewing anybody.

When dining out, one Victorian minister would not consider the occasion worth while unless he hit someone on the nose with a bread pellet.

Many years ago, a Scottish minister amused and delighted his congregation with his absent-minded habits and use of malapropisms.

He once telephoned a friend to say he was lost. 'Can you tell me where I am?' he asked.

Among his word-misuses were:

'Moses went up on Mount Cyanide to get the Ten Commandments.'

'I am worn to a fragile.'

'The Queen is laying a wreath on the cenopod.'

'I'm afraid I do make some social plunders.'

'He is someone who does not munch words.'

'Incest on the altar.'

'I have taken some milk of amnesia.'

And one New Year, he announced: 'I intend to turn into a new leaf.'

The Revd Charles Robert Maturin was mad on dancing.

He would close the shutters of his house, even if the sun was shining, and light the candles. Then, behind darkened windows, he would make believe it was a ball and dance until his feet were too sore to carry on any longer. He wore out dozens of pairs of dancing shoes every year and would also dance on carpets at friends' houses, prancing about until the carpets were threadbare.

In later years, the Revd Maturin became very absent-minded. He would arrive for parties a day late, and sometimes turned up with a boot on one foot and a dancing shoe on the other. He died in 1824 at the age of 42—after taking the wrong medicine in another absent-minded moment.

A Tennessee preacher, who died in 1850, could not have known what he looked like. From childhood he believed he would drop dead if he saw his reflection.

He never kept a mirror, and when visiting people he always asked them to remove their looking-glasses during his stay.

Richard Whately, Protestant primate of Dublin from 1831 to 1863, possessed a brilliant mind, but he could never keep still.

He was particularly jumpy while waiting for meals. A regular guest at Lord and Lady Anglesey's house in Ireland, he dislocated half a dozen chairs by whizzing them round and round on one leg while he talked.

Sometimes, bored with waiting, he would whip out a pair of scissors and trim his fingernails, or make little boomerangs out of his visiting cards and send them flying around the room.

Whately loved gardening. He would walk round his garden at least twice a day with a heavy walking stick, which had a steel blade at one end. As he walked, he lashed at weeds and lopped and pruned without interrupting his step.

He believed fresh air could cure anything. If he didn't feel well, he would go out in his shirt-sleeves, no matter how cold it was, take an axe and hack away at the toughest tree trunk he could find.

When he died of a stroke, the people of Dublin mourned. Never again would they see His Grace, the Protestant Archbishop of Dublin, striding across St Stephen's Green, working his arms round and round like a windmill, romping with his dogs and throwing pebbles at crows.

TRAVELLERS' TALES

I have ranged far for this selection of amusing tales of travelling clergymen.

A Methodist minister, retiring after many years of travel, named his new home, 'Dunmovin'.

Visiting Fremont, Nebraska, a Scottish minister found that churchmen at the city's Trinity Lutheran Church held Christmas services on June 25th. 'This is to prevent parishioners from being distracted by materialism,' smiled the Revd Craig Shultz, the pastor.

Several English clergymen touring Australia were accommodated for one night in a girls' school, which was empty because of the holidays.

One of the guests found this notice on one of the walls: 'If you require a mistress during the night, please press the bell.'

As Norfolk has only about 300 clergymen to cover 700 parishes, the Bishop of Norwich once suggested the use of motorbikes as the most economical way of getting from village to village.

'Moving with the times,' the Bishop said. 'From horses to Hondas, from gaiters to crash helmets.'

The bikes, painted blue, came into use, and the Bishop blessed them.

With the Travellers' Psalm.

A parson from South Wales, on holiday on the Greek island of Corfu, sent a card back to his church saying simply: 'Cor-phew!'

After making a journey into the West Country, the Revd James Woodforde (1740–1803) wrote in his diary: 'Accept, Oh Almighty God! my sincere and unfeigned thanks for thy great goodness to us on our late, long journey into the west and back again, and all the dangers we have escaped, particularly for that great and providential escape near Frome in Somerset. Lord! Ever make us thankful and may thy Divine Goodness ever protect us. Travelling expenses and others from the time we left Weston to our return again this evening amounted in the whole to £78.19.7d.'

On a visit to New York, an English clergyman took a yellow cab.

'There is nothing yellow about the cabs in this city,' he remarked after his harrowing ride. 'They will attack anybody.'

Dean Inge, the Dean of St Paul's Cathedral, was also a journalist.

On arrival in America, he was asked whether it was true to say that he was a pillar of the Anglican church.

'I don't know about that,' the Dean replied, 'but I am two columns in the London Evening Standard.'

Back after a trip to Malta, a vicar expressed horror at the island's chaotic traffic. 'In some places,' he said, 'they drive on the right and in others they drive on the left. In Malta, I think they tend to drive in the shade.'

HOLY ORDERS

This section is concerned with what clergymen have written in their church bulletins, and in parish newsletters and magazines. Some surprises here for those who think such publications are dull.

A parson in the Midlands pointed out in a newsletter that the Lord's Prayer has 56 words, the Ten Commandments 297, and the American Declaration of Independence 300. 'But,' he added, 'in an EEC directive on the export of duck eggs there are 26,911.'

From the Parish News of St Mary Magdalene, Latimer with Flaunden, Bucks; 'Mothers Union— sale of unwanted items. Yes, you may bring your husbands.'

The parish magazine of Priory Park Road Methodist churches in Bedford once stated: 'We are pleased to note that there has been a change of mind by the Housing Department. We did think that the naming of the new bungalows for the elderly as "St Peter's Close" was rather inappropriate.'

In a newsletter, Plymouth United Reformed Church minister, the Revd Michael Diffey, wrote that he had received from the central office of his church a card bearing the motto 'Small is beautiful'. And he added: 'It accompanied my monthly salary figure.'

A Cambridgeshire vicar quoted this report from a local newspaper in his parish magazine: 'A sudden gust of wind took all who were at the ceremony completely by surprise. Hats were blown off and copies of the vicar's speech and other rubbish were scattered over the site.'

Item in a Somerset parish magazine: 'Our great grandfathers called it the Sabbath; our fathers Sunday. Today it's known as the weekend.'

From an Irish parish magazine: 'There will be a procession next Sunday afternoon in the grounds of the monastery—but if it rains in the afternoon the procession will take place in the morning.'

This appeal appeared in the parish magazine of St Chad's Church, Chadwell Heath, Essex: 'When you were born your mother brought you here. When you were married your wife brought you here. When you die your friends will bring you here. So why not try coming on your own sometimes?'

A Cornish church letter invites you to 'Bring all your old newspapers—and your neighbours too. Please tie them up.'

A parish magazine published this item under the auspices of the vicar, the Revd C W Kirkpatrick: 'This … is … the … way … the … church … sometimes … looks … to … the … vicar … when … he … goes … into … the … pulpit.

'Wouldlooklikethisifeverbodybroughtsomebody-elsetochurch.'

One wonders whether the vicar of St George's, Weald, near Sevenoaks, Kent, made a slip or whether he put it for a joke when he compiled the list of forthcoming sermons like this:

'November 19, 10 am. Morning Praise. The Vicar: The World's Biggest Problem.'

This appeared in a Devonshire church magazine:

'Hold this square close to your face and blow on it. If it turns green, call your doctor. If it turns brown, contact your dentist. If it turns purple, see a psychiatrist. If it turns red, see your bank manager. If it turns black, call your solicitor and make a will. If it remains the same colour, you are in good health, and there is no reason on earth why you should not be in church next Sunday morning.'

Printed in a church magazine: 'Pot luck supper. Prayer and medication follow.'

Whoops, another slip is showing in this Huntingdonshire parish newspaper: 'The Sunday

School barbecue will be held on Friday evening. At least two adults will be pleasant all evening.'

From the Dubai parish magazine, *Palm Leaves*: 'The concert was a great success. Special thanks are due to the vicar's daughter who laboured the whole evening at the piano, which as usual fell upon her.'

This item appeared in an American church magazine: 'The Revd Jarvis has spoken in the largest Baptist churches in the USA. To miss hearing him will be the chance of a lifetime.'

From a parish newsletter: 'Miss Marcia Devlin sang "I will not pass this way again" to the obvious delight of the entire congregation.'

THE SPORTING TYPES

Many clergymen enjoy playing sport—but not all take it seriously. So their game is often laced with humour.

Soccer-mad vicars in Preston, Lancashire, played a football match in the middle of the night, dressed in clerical black, to raise money for charity.

Why the dead of night? So no one could see how bad they were!

In order to get fit for a squash match, a middle-aged vicar from South Wales tried dieting. After a fortnight, he announced: 'I've been on this diet for two weeks, and all I've lost is fourteen days.'

The vicar liked to play at centre forward. 'I'm known as Neckline Noonan,' he said. 'Plunging down the middle, but never really showing much.'

Badly beaten by an elderly parishioner, a golfing parson in Hampshire returned glumly to the clubhouse.

'Cheer up,' said his opponent. 'Remember, you will win eventually. You will be burying me one day.'

'Yes,' replied the parson, 'but even then it will be your hole.'

A young vicar in the West Country, who plays in goal for a junior football club on Saturdays, cheerfully admits that he is known as 'Cinderella'.

When asked why, he replies: 'Because I keep missing the ball.'

A vicar on holiday in Wales, went for a round of golf on a local course.

The secretary of the club, coming out of the clubhouse, noted the clergyman placing the ball carefully about a foot ahead of the markers on the first tee. Fairly politely, the secretary pointed out that the rules stated the ball must be placed in a certain position, but *not* in front of the markers.

The vicar thanked him for the advice, then added with as much dignity as he could sum up: 'But you see, I am about to play my *second shot*.'

Heard on a golf course, one clergyman to another who had overshot a hole: 'Why, Leonard, your putt runneth over.'

In Surrey, a vicar who turns out for the church hockey team had this to say after his side's fourteenth successive defeat: 'The trouble with being a good sport is that you have to lose to prove it.'

When the Revd R Dilwyn Edwards was a Methodist probationer minister in Launceston, Cornwall, he preached in the pulpit on Sunday and played for the local football team on Saturday. And he used to say, 'I have full faith in my team secretary.'

Whose name happened to be John Wesley.

A cricket-mad clergyman in the Midlands was still playing the game in his fifties, and he tended to talk in the clubhouse after the match of his accomplishments when younger.

Then, one afternoon, noting an expression of

scepticism on the face of one member, he interrupted himself in full flow: 'Actually, it's funny—the older I get, the better I used to be.'

The scene: a village cricket match down in deepest Devon.

The vicar makes his way to the wicket, takes guard and is bowled middle stump first ball.

As he makes his way sadly back to the clubhouse, his wife, who knows nothing about the game, turns to her friend and says: 'Oh, look, isn't it just like Edwin to forget something.'

Dr Robert Runcie, former Archbishop of Canterbury, revealed on a television programme that playing soccer, cricket and tennis as a young man helped to prepare him for later life.

'I played them all by myself,' he said, 'against a very good wall.'

A portly Sussex vicar took up with cross country running with a much thinner colleague.

One bitterly cold winter morning, as they started off on their run, the vicar glanced at his friend, who was shivering, and remarked: 'You're shivering, my friend. Your shivers are the wages of thin.'

'I play Second War golf,' a parson was heard to remark in a clubhouse in Surrey. 'You know, out in 39 and back in 45.'

After spraining his right wrist during a table tennis game, a Cambridgeshire parson revealed: 'I would give my right arm to be ambidextrous.'

The vicar was taking golf lessons.

'Now,' said the pro, 'suppose you just go through the motions without driving the ball.'

'Ah,' the vicar replied, 'but, you see, that is precisely the difficulty I'm trying to overcome.'

And the same clergyman was heard to say at one point to his instructor, 'Now you *must* tell me if you see me doing anything right.'

On a tennis court in Newquay, a visiting player—a clergyman from London—confessed to being at the veteran stage. 'Tennis is certainly a great reducer,' he commented. 'My shorts come in three sizes—June, July and August.'

WIT'S END

Even a long and serious sermon can be brightened with a whiff of real humour. I present a collection of charmingly witty epigrams made by clergymen up in the pulpit.

Here is what the chaplain of Girton, Cambridgeshire, said at his Ascension Day service one year: 'We light the candle at the front of the chapel to symbolise Christ's physical presence on earth. And to symbolise his departure to heaven, one of the chapel wardens goes up to the front and snuffs it.'

A Surrey vicar announced: 'Children are normally collected during the offertory hymn.'

Asked to keep his sermon short one week, a clergyman in Texas said: 'Hi—bye.'

A minister, who always reads his sermons, one day placed his text on the pulpit about half-an-hour before the service. But a young member of the congregation surreptitiously removed the last page of the manuscript.

Preaching away vigorously, the minister came to the words: 'So Adam said to Eve ...' Turning the page, he was horrified to discover that the final page was missing. He gained a little time by repeating: 'Yes, Adam said to Eve ...' Then his face broke into a big smile.

'I'm afraid there seems to be a leaf missing ...'

'I hope my sermon last week was not too long,' said a Wiltshire vicar. 'I mention this because I hear one small boy said to his father at one stage, "When the red light turns green, can we move on?"'

The vicar was, of course, referring to the red glow of the sanctuary lamp over the altar!

Said a vicar to his congregation: 'Earlier this morning I felt rather depressed. But now, as I face you, I feel I am experiencing one of the little joys of my job. I am thinking, I am able to speak at some length, uninterrupted, on any subject I choose—and my wife and my children are going to sit there, say nothing and listen.'

In Kentucky, a black parson denounced certain members of his congregation for 'putting on airs'.

He then put on an exaggerated accent and shouted: 'Some folks reminds me of de bottom figger of a fraction. De bigger dey try to be, de smaller dey really is.'

A vicar in Birmingham announced solemnly. 'I have been asked to point out that the University's Extra Mural Courses start at 7.30 pm, with the subject being *Approaches to God*. You may apply to me for transport arrangements.'

'I really do not mind if someone looks at his watch during my sermon,' said a London vicar. 'What upsets me is when he takes it off and shakes it to see if it is still going.'

A Cornish vicar told his congregation that there are more than 700 different sins. 'And,' he added, 'after last week's sermon I received a couple of requests for the list!'

In Preston, a vicar said that a lady's watch had been found in a pew. 'It may be claimed in the vestry after the service,' he said. He paused before announcing the closing hymn. 'It will be, "Lord Her Watch Thy Church is Keeping".'

The Revd Robert Yeomans of Pontesbury, Shropshire, tried to instil more zest into his choir during a rendering of 'I Wonder Where I'm Bound'. So he bounced up and down. Unfortunately, the grid under him gave way and the Revd Yeomans dropped straight into the church's central heating duct.

As he got up, he brought the church down by crying: '*Now* I know where I'm bound!'

The vicar was not optimistic about the present state of the world. 'If Moses came down from the Mount now,' he said, 'the two tablets he'd carry would probably be aspirin.'

After the church's junior choir had finished singing, the vicar made his way up to the pulpit. When he got there, he noticed one young singer walking out.

'Mmm,' the vicar observed, 'I suppose he's used to leaving the room during the commercials.'

A vicar in the Midlands was commenting on the contemporary architecture of a new church. 'I honestly don't know whether to pray *in* it or *for* it,' he said.

Said a North country vicar: 'People these days seem to get so nostalgic about things they weren't so happy about the first time round.'

Before the service one Sunday morning, the American cleric Henry Ward Beecher was handed a note containing a single word: Fool.

He described the note to his congregation like this:

'I have known many instances of a man writing a letter and forgetting to sign his name. But this is the first case I have ever known of a man signing his name and forgetting to write the letter.'

71

'The next hymn is the one the serpent sang to Eve,' announced a North London vicar to his congregation: 'A Bite With Me'.

It was a cold, wet Sunday morning, and the vicar started his sermon by saying: 'Today I got up at the crack of dawn, stuffed up the crack and went back to bed ...'

This was the closing prayer by a black pastor, after an over-garnished sermon by a visiting brother: 'We thank Thee, Lawd, fo' ouah brother and fo' his ministry. But oh, Lawd, help him to take a few feathahs out of the wings of his imagination and stick them in the tail of his judgement!'

'When I first made my sermons many years ago,' a Norfolk vicar said solemnly, 'I wished I had a voice as resonant and penetrating as some in the congregation who whisper.'

From Canada, this little story:

The church service and the Sunday school classes were both held from 10 to 11am. One Sunday the six- to eight-year-olds were dismissed early, and they headed for the lobby to wait for their parents. All except one—the minister's small son.

The child raced through the lobby and down the aisle, behind the wheel of an imaginary racing car, providing his own sound effects at the top of his lungs. 'Varoom! Screech!' he yelled, as he leaned into a hairpin turn into the front row pew and collapsed next to his embarrassed mother.

Undeterred by this, the boy's father interrupted his sermon just long enough to say: 'Park it, Phillip, and give the keys to your mother.'

During the solemn Ash Wednesday service in the cathedral, the Revd John Venus of Fareham, Hampshire, discovered that by mistake he had been given a robe meant for a much taller cleric.

He hitched the spare linen above the girdle, but as he climbed up the steps his foot caught in the hem and there was a most embarrassing sound of cloth being torn.

Then, reading from the prayer book, the Revd Venus said: 'Rend your heart and not your garments.'

After making a special appeal for funds for the missions, the preacher ended by saying: 'Those who smoke are asked to give the price of twenty cigarettes. Those who drink, the price of a double whisky. Those who swear, ten pence for every swear word used since last Sunday. And those who do not smoke, drink or swear are asked to wrap up their haloes in a five pound note and put that in the collection.'

After completing his sermon, a vicar made reference to the new Young Mother's Group. 'If any of the young women in our church would like to become young mothers,' he said, 'would they please come and see me in the vestry later.'

CLASSIC QUOTES

Essentially brief, the best quote will demonstrate wit or wisdom, or both, and make its point without explanation or preamble. So digest now a selection of humorous and thought-provoking pronouncements from men of the cloth.

'I am just a few minutes old.'

Cockney George Carey, on becoming Archbishop of Canterbury to a peal of bells at the ceremony of St Mary-le-Bow in East London.

'Sentimentality is no indication of a warm heart. Nothing weeps more copiously than a chunk of ice.'

An Australian minister

'One of the great virtues of a modern pop song is that you know it can't last.'

The Revd C R Cloutier

'I know what the world is coming to eventually. I just wonder what it's coming to in the meantime.'
   American preacher Raymond Wilson

'Some forgetfulness is due not to absent-mindedness but to absent-heartedness.'
   The Revd Isaac Rottenberg

'A Christian is someone who feels repentance on a Sunday for what he did on Saturday and is going to do on Monday.'
   The Revd Thomas Yeara in *The Christian*

'It is admirable for a man to take his son fishing, but there is a special place in heaven for the father who takes his daughter shopping.'
   The Revd William McGhee

'I am only controversial among people who don't share my views.'
   An Oxfordshire clergyman

'When I get to heaven I hope to meet the people to finish the conversations that were interrupted at cocktail parties.'
    The Revd Sydney Thomas

'Blessed are they who hunger and thirst—they must be sticking to their diets.'
    The Revd Leonard Berkow

'When I was little, I suppose you could have called me a "Venial Sin." But after I die, people will realise I was a "Mortal Sin". And all are welcome to "The House of Sin".'
    Cardinal Jaime Sin

'Though I am always in haste, I am never in a hurry.'
    John Wesley

'A saint is a sinner who keeps on trying.'
    A New York clergyman

'Utility is when you possess one telephone, luxury is when you have two, opulence is when you have three—and paradise is when you have none.'
  A preacher in Virginia, USA

'Enthusiasm is the yeast that can make your hopes and dreams rise to the stars.'
  The Revd Robert Harper

'The secret of a good sermon is a good beginning and a good ending—and not having them too far apart.'
  A New South Wales clergyman

'The first time I ever heard an archbishop, I remember my father saying, "Unctuous old humbug!" My father was such a good man and I try to remember his remark when I am speaking. I think all over the country there are lovely people saying, "Unctuous old humbug!" It's a good corrective.'
  Dr Robert Runcie, Archbishop of Canterbury

'Unhappiness in my view is not knowing what we want and killing ourselves in our desire to get it.'
   D M Apple, American clergyman

'Tact is kindness with a brain.'
   The Revd Morton Robinson

'God has promised forgiveness to your repentance, but he has not promised tomorrow to your procrastination.'
   St Augustine

'The main purpose of eloquence seems to be to prevent other people from saying something.'
   The Revd Charles S Kause

'Every year it takes less time to fly across the ocean and longer to get to church.'
   The Revd Allan Walker

'May the Good Lord receive ye—but not too soon.'
   Father Francis Patrick Duffy

'American Indians used to send messages by holding a wet blanket over the fire. Now we have television and get to see the wet blanket in person.'
   A North Dakota minister

'Originality is undetected plagiarism.'
   Dean W R Inge

'When the missionaries first came to Africa, they had the Bible and we had the land. They said, "Let us pray." We closed our eyes, and when we opened them, the tables had been turned: we had the Bible and they had the land.'
   Desmond Tutu, Bishop of Johannesburg and winner of 1984 Nobel peace prize

'Adam was the only man who could not use the line, "Haven't we met before somewhere?"'
  A New York cleric

'Beautiful young people are accidents of nature. But beautiful old people are works of art.'
  American minister Roscoe J Brown

'A reformer is someone who insists upon his conscience being your guide.'
  The Revd Millard Miller

'The departure of the Three Wise Men from the East seems to have been on a more extensive scale than is generally supposed, for no one of that description seems to have been left behind.'
  The Revd Sydney Smith

'Horse power was a whole lot safer when the horses had it.'
  A Tennessee preacher

MISCELLANY

This final section contains a miscellany of stories from here, there and everywhere to illustrate just how funny clerics in today's society can be.

The Revd Handley, curate of Christ Church, Ashton-under-Lyme, Lancashire, once stood in the local market place collecting donations for the Church of England Children's Society.

His plea to shoppers: 'Wife and 5,000 children to support.'

A country parson was fond of saying: 'The Bible is my one and only reverence book.'

At a theological college, it was the custom to vary the canticles and psalms at the morning service from day to day.

Announcing the 'Te Deum' one morning, the rather absent-minded principal began by saying brightly, 'We praise Thee O God ...' He then quickly corrected himself, saying, 'Oh no we don't—it's Friday!'

Vicar John Haynes amazed his congregation in Warwickshire by handing out fistfuls of fivers. He told them to follow the Bible parable of the talents, and use the money to create even more cash. Then he asked them to hand over the total to help send a cow to a poor family in Uganda.

In Newbury, Berkshire, a vicar, driving his car, nearly knocked a cyclist over.

They stopped and had a friendly chat. Then the vicar pulled out one of his calling cards. 'I feel I must give you this,' he said.

The card read: 'The Reverend Smith is sorry he missed you today.'

A small boy asked a vicar in North Devon what was meant by the fast days.

'When you have to eat in a hurry, my son,' the vicar replied.

A Surrey clergyman had a reputation for unsolicited criticism of the generosity of his host at local functions.

Asked to say grace, he would quickly scan the table. If the cutlery was limited to a knife, fork and spoon, his oblation would begin: 'For the least of these Thy mercies.'

But a full place setting would evoke an enthusiastic: 'O most bountiful Giver.'

On the day of an annual church outing in St Neots, Huntingdonshire, rain was falling heavily and the roads were becoming flooded.

As the first coach left, the vicar raised his hands. 'God bless this coach,' he said, 'and all who sail in her today.'

A Leicestershire vicar, who had been waiting over a fortnight for a painter and decorator to call, finally sent him a note with a Bible reference on it.

Puzzled, the man looked up Matthew 11:3 and read: 'Art thou he that should come, or do we look for another?'

The work was done the following day.

A clergyman in South London likes to recall the time he attended a church social evening in Streatham. 'And,' he says, 'would you believe it, there were three guests there called Bean, Gawne and Dunnit!'

After being given a most flowery introduction to his speech, a clergyman rose to his feet and beamed. 'May the Lord forgive this man for his excesses— and me for enjoying them so much.'

Canon Neil Pritchard, vicar of Holy Trinity Church, Blackpool, used to answer his telephone with the first two words of the church's name.

But he stopped when his bishop responded: 'How nice to get through without saying one's prayers!'

A vicar and father of a young family was always trying to cut expenses. One afternoon, while out shopping with his wife, he saw that she had put an anniversary card for him in her basket.

He picked out the card, read it carefully and said: 'Why, thank you so much, my dear.' Then he put the card back on the shelf.

Episcopal bishop James Pike, a former practising lawyer, was asked why he gave up the law.

'I didn't,' he replied. 'I merely changed clients.'

'The bishop and I never clash,' a young parson declared. 'He goes his way and I go his.'

When it was announced that the prebendary of St Paul's Cathedral, Peter Ball, was to be promoted, one cleric observed: 'He will be Canon Ball—and clearly the right calibre for the job.'

The Revd Philip Randall, now retired from the parish of Eye, Peterborough, admits that he spent eight years searching the Parish Register for a name to match the initials HWP on a stone slab in his church.

Then, one day, he found out what they stand for—Hot Water Pipe.

According to one vicar, parishioners are sometimes stuck for something to say to him following the service. What has been said includes:

'We really shouldn't make you preach so often.'

'You always manage to find something to say to fill in the time.'

'I don't care what other people may say—*I* like your sermons.'

'Did you know there are 243 panes of glass in those windows?'

'If I'd known you were going to be so good today, I'd have brought my neighbour with me.'

The hospital chaplain always carried a pocket pager, an electronic device that notified him when he was needed.

One day he visited a woman patient, who asked him to pray with her. As he intoned, 'Dear Lord', the device in his pocket went 'beep, beep, beep'.

Noting the look of puzzlement on the patient's face, the chaplain said: 'Direct contact, you see.'

When the rector invited some theology students to tea, they were determined to follow what he did.

And when the rector poured milk into his saucer, the students did likewise.

But then the clergyman leaned down and placed his saucer on the floor.

For his cat.

A clergyman who was taking a theological class told the young men that the subject of the next lecture would be the sin of deceit and that, by way of preparation, he wanted them to read the 17th chapter of St Mark's Gospel.

A day or so later, he asked the class how many had read that chapter thoroughly. Everyone raised a hand.

'Thank you,' the cleric said. 'It is to people such as yourselves that this morning's lecture is especially addressed. There is no 17th chapter of Mark.'

The Crown Princess (later Queen) Louise of Sweden once visited Uppsala Cathedral.

The archbishop, keen to demonstrate his knowledge of English, approached a chest of drawers in the sacristy and made this interesting announcement: 'I will now open these trousers and reveal some even more precious treasures to Your Royal Highness.'

Here's an enterprising clergyman. Rector Donald Allister advertises his church on 2,000 beer mats in local pubs at Cheadle, Greater Manchester—to try and attract more regulars.

A priest in Arequipa, Peru, complained that a fellow priest had brought a surge of popularity to the ritual of confession. 'I sometimes wait an hour for someone to come and confess, but penitents form long queues to tell everything to my colleague.'

There was an explanation: the other priest was deaf.

In Maryland, USA, a preacher called Virgil, with a wife called Mary, wrote to his local newspaper to say that some people referred to them as 'Virg and Mary'.

After the senior men's group in the church, all over sixty, formed a small band to play a mixture of country, soul and religious music, the minister named the group: 'Rock of Ages'.

A retired priest recalls this story.

As he was becoming rather deaf, and as people tend to whisper in the confessional, he asked those who came to him to write their sins on a sheet of paper and hand them over.

'This worked quite well,' he said. 'Then one day a lady handed me a slip bearing the message, "Tea, $\frac{1}{2}$lb butter, 2lb sugar, cheese". We could only reflect on the list of sins she had left with her grocer!'

Pasadena Community Church, St Petersburg, was the first to introduce the 'drive-in church' in America, to accommodate the immense overflow crowd.

In hundreds of cars, churchgoers heard the

minister boom over the loudspeaker: 'Honk your horns once for amen, and twice for hallelujah!'

A clergyman was stopped on a country road for speeding. He told the policeman that he was in a great hurry because he had so many things to attend to. 'After all,' he said, 'I'm on this earth to do God's work.

'And,' he added, 'I suppose that is why you are here too.'

Noting the policeman's bemused expression, the cleric explained: 'Remember that part of the Bible which says, "Go out into the highways and hedges and compel them to come in."'

A priest in charge of a church says the oddest thing he ever found in the collection plate was a biscuit wrapped in paper. It was marked: 'For the poor church mouse.'

In South Carolina, USA, a preacher called Clarence Massey formed the 'Clarence Anti-Defamation

League', with the object of stopping people form making fun of his name.

A Lancashire vicar who inadvertently locked himself inside his parish church rang out SOS in Morse code on the church bell.

He was rescued by a Girl Guide.

After hearing his first confession, a young curate went to the elderly priest and said: 'Tell me, Father, how did I do?'

The priest thought for a moment, then said: 'My son, you did rather well. But I have one suggestion—when you hear the confessions of these pretty young women, it would be a bit more seemly if you went "Tsk, tsk, tsk!" and not "Wheewww!"'

Dalesman

Whitby

HARRY COLLETT

Dalesman

Dalesman Publishing Company Ltd
Stable Courtyard, Broughton Hall,
Skipton, North Yorkshire BD23 3AZ
www.dalesman.co.uk

First Edition 2000, Reprinted 2003

Text © Harry Collett
Illustrations © John Freeman, Market Place, Whitby

Maps by Jeremy Ashcroft and Harry Salisbury

Cover: Whitby from High Bridge by Alan Curtis

A British Library Cataloguing in Publication record
is available for this book

ISBN 1 85568 174 9

Printed by Amadeus Press, Cleckheaton

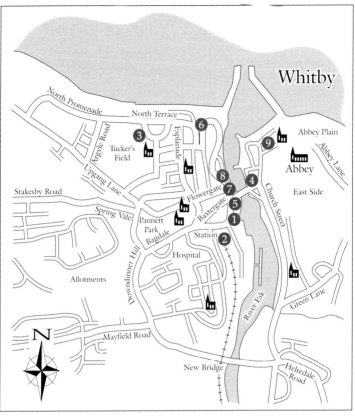

Whitby

Introduction

A thousand years of ecclesiastical and maritime heritage are preserved in the historic port of Whitby. Situated at the heart of Yorkshire's stunning Heritage Coast where, between lofty cliffs, the River Esk finds its way into the North Sea, it remains isolated by the rugged hills, moors and dales of the North York Moors National Park.

High on the windswept East Cliff the remains of the 13th century Abbey dominate the skyline, dwarfing the Church of St Mary with its adjacent graveyard, from which a flight of 199 stairs descend into the old town – an irregular jumble of red tiled cottages, narrow yards, ghauts (alleyways which run from the street onto the riverside) and cobbled streets. The call of the gulls, the smell of the sea and outstanding views of the twin stone piers are constant reminders of the town's maritime links.

The River Esk divides the town into two halves linked by a wrought iron swing bridge over the tidal harbour, with its fishing boats, cargo ships, yachts, pleasure craft and the orange and blue coloured lifeboat.

High on the West Cliff stands a statue of Whitby's most famous adopted son, Captain Cook, famed for his great voyages of exploration in ships built in local boatyards and launched into the river below. Nearby the huge jawbones of a whale recall Whitby's heyday as a whaling port.

It was the pioneering 'Railway King' George Hudson who brought the railways into Whitby. He developed the West Cliff, building rows of sturdy boarding houses, the Royal Hotel and half of a splendid Royal Crescent. His money ran out before he had time to complete it, but Whitby owes him much for opening up the town as a tourist destination.

When we tread the streets and byways of the town today, we tread the same routes taken by generations long gone. Routes that have remained unchanged, despite the changing phases of the town's development since medieval times.

With the passage of time, the narrow streets became thronged with landlubbers and cosmopolitan faces from ships newly arrived in the harbour from Russia and the Americas; whalers home from their dangerous activities in Spitsbergen, reeking of whale blubber; grimy sailors off collier cats, mingling with wealthy merchants and craftsmen who worked in the bustling noisy ship-building yards.

Whitby represents every period of history. The Romans knew it as Streoneshalh or 'Sinus Fari' which the scholar Bede translated as 'The bay of the ·Lighthouse'. Following the Viking raiders and their colonisation of the Esk Valley, the settlers renamed the town 'Hviteby' meaning white town. By the 18th century it was the seventh most important port in England thanks to its tonnage of registered wooden, sail-driven ships.

Small enough to be walked around, Whitby's unique charm offers something vastly different from other seaside resorts. But Whitby does not live in the past, only thrives on it; for people come from all over the world to relish the romance of the past and find the Whitby of the present.

For Whitby binds us to herself, we folk who love her well.

PUBLISHER'S NOTE

The information given in this book has been provided in good faith and is intended only as a general guide. Whilst all reasonable efforts have been made to ensure that details were correct at the time of publication, the author and Dalesman Publishing Company Ltd cannot accept any responsibility for inaccuracies. It is the responsibility of individuals undertaking outdoor activities to approach the activity with caution and, especially if inexperienced, to do so under appropriate supervision. They should also carry the appropriate equipment and maps, be properly clothed and have adequate footwear. The sport described in this book is strenuous and individuals should ensure that they are suitably fit before embarking upon it.

Upper east side

Pressmen and mariners

The walk is about 2 miles and takes about 1¹/₂ hours.
Start and finish at the swing bridge

There has been a river crossing near to this spot since early times. The ford, with its sandstone blocks, was just below the present bridge. The earliest recorded bridge, 1351, was replaced in 1578. Its replacement in 1766 cost £3,000 and was a drawbridge – the leaves, when raised, often got caught in the sail ships' rigging.

Cross the bridge and on your right is the **Dolphin Hotel**. Originally a coffee house it soon gravitated into the Custom House Hotel, later to be used as a rendezvous for naval sea captains whose instructions from the Admiralty were "to collect men for the service of the crown". One of the deceptions used was to drop a 'shilling' into a tankard of ale. Having quaffed the ale, the coin became visible and was fished out. Once flesh had touched the coin, the drinker was deemed to have accepted the 'King's shilling' and had 'volunteered' to serve in the Royal Navy! Those unfortunates were kept chained together in the cellars before being shipped out to sea.

In **Grape Lane** many of the buildings date from the 17th, 18th and 19th centuries. A tall building halfway along on the right was a former bank and has the largest 'bottle' window in town. Built at the time when window tax was enforced on property, rather than pay for a window on each of the four landings, one window was extended the height of the building thus saving some 75 per cent of the tax.

Next door the old hospital has become the Pictorial Archives Centre. The last building in the lane on the right dates from 1619. The house was altered for Moses and Susannah Dring in 1688. It was later

The Swing Bridge

FREEMAN 00

purchased by John Walker, a Master Mariner. A Quaker by religion, he also taught young men the service of the sea, one of whom was James Cook, who having served a three year apprenticeship was employed for a further five years on Walker's ships, becoming a friend for life. After joining the Royal Navy, Cook achieved fame as a navigator and explorer with his three great voyages of discovery.

At the junction with Grape Lane and **Church Street** the 'Thingwald' or council of Danish Whitby met. The cobbled area is all that remains of the Potato Market, where prior to 1540 stood the Tollgate where the Abbot of Whitby exacted his dues.

Down Church Street on the left is the **Seamen's Hospital** founded in 1670 to cater for retired mariners and their dependants. The present frontage was designed by Sir Gilbert Scott in 1842 with stone mullions. The figure head of the Black Prince adorns the niche above the main entrance and, above that, interesting carvings are set below a model ship.

7

Further along Church Street is a narrow opening called **Salt Pan Well Steps** where, in the seventeenth century, Sir Hugh Cholmley started a salt industry. Climb the steps. The yard contained a pump, since removed to Whitby Museum, erected by William Scoresby, the famous whaler and Arctic navigator, and which bore the inscription, "To everyone his own, Draw, Drink, Be Silent." William Scoresby (the elder) invented the ice drill and the lookout known as the 'crow's nest', afterwards adopted by all whaling ships. He also sailed in 1806 in a wooden sail ship to the highest latitude approaching the North Pole.

At the top of the steps, you are now on **The Ropery**, one of three in the town which provided rigging for the shipbuilding industry. The large building to the right, now St Hilda's Business Centre, was the Union Workhouse.

Turning left, the high wall blocks out the view of the first workhouse erected in 1727. When the Union was built on The Ropery in 1792 the old workhouse was converted into tenements by shipowner Gideon Smales.

At the end of the wall descend the ramp onto the cobbled way named **Boulby Bank**. The monks who moved goods around the county on the backs of ponies and packhorses laid down trods (sandstone blocks end to end) to prevent the beasts getting foot-rot. There are still 127 miles of these trods or medieval motorways in North Yorkshire. Follow the trod up the rise on your right, between the cottages.

The view from the gallery above the Seamen's Hospital gives panoramic vistas across the town and harbour before, on your left, you come to **Elbow Terrace** where it is said that before these new buildings were erected a tunnel ran from Church Street into Elbow Yard for use by smugglers.

The lane follows the route to the corner of the '**Donkey field**' where horses, ponies and donkeys having shed their panniers were allowed to graze and drink from the spring in the centre of the field. In 1634 Sir Hugh Cholmley culverted the well to provide drinking

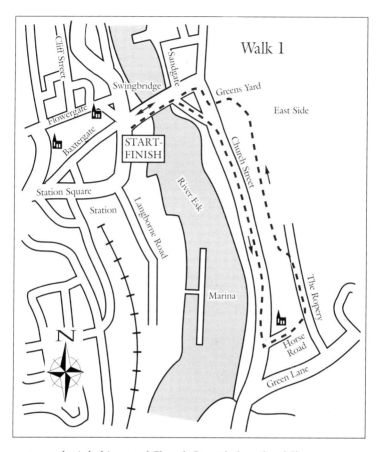

Walk 1

water to the inhabitants of Church Street below the cliff.

Descending the stairs to your left, you emerge in Greens Yard and out onto Church Street. Opposite is a row of medieval town houses with overhanging upper storeys. Next door is the Friends' Meeting House, the place of worship for the Quakers of the town who were very influential in providing finance for the development of shipbuilding – particularly the coal-carrier barks known as 'Collier Cats'.

Next door is a shop which sells jet, the fossilised wood of the Monkey Puzzle tree from the Jurassic period 160 million years ago. The use of

9

jet for personal adornment dates back some 6,000 years when as a talisman it was believed to give protection from the evil eye and that dreaded disease leprosy.

Jet gets its earliest written mention in Whitby in 1394, when an Abbot left a set of rosary beads to his Benedictine brother in a will. The fashion for ornaments and jewellery made from Whitby Jet reached its zenith in the nineteenth century when Queen Victoria's husband Prince Albert the Consort died and the monarch required black jewellery for mourning.

The Great Exhibition at Crystal Palace in 1851 gave the Whitby Jet trade an international boost. Exhibits on display from local craftsmen were valued at £90,000 and provided employment for almost nine hundred workers. Jet is currently undergoing a revival, particularly in Japan and the Far East.

The fine building on the corner is a 14th century three-decker merchants' house which leads into **Bridge Street** and the approach to the swing bridge.

Lower west side

Shipbuilders and smugglers

Approximately 1¹/₂ miles in length and takes about 1¹/₄ hours.
Start at the Railway Station. Finish at the swing bridge .

By the turn of the 18th century, the heyday of wooden ships was finished. Wood was replaced by steel and sail by steam and this area was reclaimed from the tidal mudflats and shipyards. One shipyard site now hosts the railway station, built in 1847 for George Hudson the 'Railway King' to a design by G.T. Andrews. **New Quay Road** housed the shipyard of Jarvis Coates, whilst along the river bank, upstream, stood the yards of Coates, Barry, Barrick and Thomas Fishburn where Captain James Cook's ship *Endeavour* was built. When launched she was named the *Earl of Pembroke* and was a collier cat, until bought by the Admiralty in 1768 and refitted for Cook's first voyage of discovery.

Turn left into **Station Square,** once Thomas Hutchinson's ship repair yard. On the left the Coliseum (1887), a former Temperance Hall, Cinema and Bingo palace, is now a Network Centre. Opposite, Boyes store was formerly a cinema until 1983. A century ago Bagdale Beck, now culverted, flowed between these buildings and one could fish from the paddock where now stand estate agents' and solicitors' offices. The beck was so deep that stones used in the building of the west pier were floated down on mini-barges.

On the left a narrow entrance to **Spring Hill** leads to Whitby Hospital and the Police Station. At the junction with Spring Hill stands **Bagdale Hall.** Built in Tudor times for James Conyers, Sergeant at Arms to Henry the VIII, the house passed into the hands of the Bushell family. Captain Browne Bushell was a prominent local character during the drama of the Civil War and he changed sides many times during the hostilities. Eventually, revolting from Parliament with a good ship, he turned pirate, was apprehended and following trial suffered the death penalty on 29th March 1651.

Continuing up Bagdale is **Broomfield Terrace,** at the rear of which is a small circular building with a lantern roof. This is the **Victorian Spa**, the waters of which were drunk as a remedy for anaemia and other ailments. On the opposite side of the road is the Quaker Burial Ground. Adjoining is a terrace of houses where Capt. Scoresby lived following his retirement from whaling.

The Endeavour

Retracing your steps take the zebra crossing into **Victoria Square,** or Trinity Corner as was, you find St Hilda's Catholic Church on one corner, the Anglican Church of St John on the other and, up **Brunswick Street**, between them Brunswick Methodist Chapel. Brunswick Street was originally Skate Lane. Here the fishermen laid out the fish named skate to dry on its south facing slope, before the days of refrigeration.

Baxtergate is built upon sandbanks by the river estuary and in the 18th century shops and factories mingled with residential dwellings.

First right after Boyes store is **Beck Yard** and next to it **Linskill Yard**, named after Reuben Linskill, who was

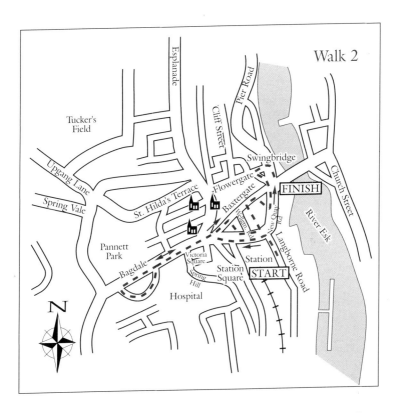

connected with the alum trade. He built houses in his rear garden which led onto the riverside for the alum workers. (Alum was used as the mordant in the dyeing of wool, and for softening leather.) This cobbled Georgian gem leads back into Station Square.

Turn left and cross Wellington Road. On the left is **Loggerhead Yard** and the Tap & Spile Pub. When the public house, under a different name, had a river frontage, smuggled goods were brought in and passed through a tunnel which ran underneath the cottages, the length of Loggerhead Yard, into the then Ship Launch Inn. Originally the hostelry was known as The Green Man and dated back to AD1401 when Baxtergate was a residential street. It has been again renamed The Smugglers Café.

Back now in Baxtergate, called after the Baxter family who owned most of the property there until 1700, a number of buildings midway along attract our interest.

On the left enter Johnsons and Lengs yard and view the artisan's cottage on the left. Contrast it with the large house opposite in Baxtergate, now a solicitor's office. This fine building was the private residence for Jarvis Coates, shipbuilder. Opposite is the Church of St Ninian. Opened in 1778 and still owned by descendants of the original proprietors, it contains the original three-sided gallery and carved front.

Turn right down a narrow alley into **New Quay Road**. On the left is The Angel Hotel, scene of Georgian public assemblies and cockfights. The first stagecoach entered into Angel yard in 1775. Twenty years later the 'Whitby Neptune' made the journey to Leeds carrying the mail in ten-and-a-half hours. Perhaps the most important meeting at the Angel took place in 1832 when George Stephenson discussed with local worthies the building of a horse-drawn railway to either Pickering or Stockton. Pickering was selected and when the line was opened in 1836 a great procession marched from the Angel to the original railway station, near the Bog Hall signal box.

Opposite the Swing Bridge is **Golden Lion Bank**. The small open area was, up to 1640, the market place before Lord Cholmey moved the market place over to the east side, and had built the Town Hall. The Golden Lion Public House, one of the three major inns in the town, was sold in 1714 with "the sign of the Golden Lion and the post on which it stands". Close by in the 17th century stood the town stocks.

At the top of the bank is the **Sutcliffe Gallery** featuring the world renowned work of Victorian photographer Frank Sutcliffe. To its right stands the old Flowergate Chapel which has been Unitarian since 1695.

Cross the road and the lane on the right leads back down to the harbour side. **St Ann's Lane** used to be known as 'Hells Lane'. It led to a raised set of stepping stones across the river. When the tide was rising and the wind blew strong then it was hell getting across the river to the east side.

Turn right at the bottom and retrace your steps on New Quay Road. Look up and see the carving on the National Westminster Bank. On the HSBC Bank building opposite are more carvings and a blue plaque which recalls that in the first fleet, transporting convicts to Botany Bay, two of the eleven-strong convoy, the *Fishburn* and the *Golden Grove*, were Whitby-built.

Skate Lane – now
Brunswick Street

In search of Dracula

2 miles in length and takes about 1¹/₂ hours.
Start in Royal Crescent, West Cliff. Finish top of the 199 stairs

In 1893 the Irish Author, Abraham (Bram) Stoker, visited Whitby for a holiday. He was employed as business manager to Sir Henry Irving's theatre company and was intent on writing a play for his employer which would give him lasting glory. What he found in Whitby was to prove rather exceptional and would ultimately take six years to plan, research and write. It came to fruition in 1897, but Sir Henry Irving rejected it, causing Stoker to rewrite it as a novel. When published under the title *Dracula* it became an instant success.

The old Town Hall

Start in **Royal Crescent**, West Cliff, at no 6, where a blue plaque denotes the house where Stoker stayed on his visits to Whitby. Go onto the seafront and turning right you come to the Royal Hotel. It contains in the foyer a photographic portrait of Bram Stoker and a print by Frank Sutcliffe of the Russian Ship that ran aground on Tate Hill Sands, some years before Stoker published his novel.

Turning right along East Terrace you come to **East Crescent**. In one of the nine houses, the heroines of the story – Mina and Lucy – are on holiday. At no 7 lives the lawyer engaged by Count

Dracula to transport his strange cargo from Transylvania – fifty coffins of common earth.

From this point you can view the graveyard of St Mary's Church, the large house Streonshalh not having been built until after Stoker's death. Descend the steps and go down the Khyber Pass. On the right, climb the steps onto **Spion Kop**.

At the southern end of the Spion Kop is a wrought iron and wood Victorian-style seat which commemorates the link between the author and the town, and the inspiration he derived while writing chapters 6-8 of *Dracula*. The seat looks directly across the harbour to the East Cliff – both cliffs provide settings for episodes in the story – and from it you can see every feature of the town mentioned in the novel.

Retrace your steps and follow the road to the bottom of the Khyber Pass where it curves to join Pier Road. Having glimpsed Lucy in the moonlight, Mina races along the fish quay in a desperate bid to reach her. Her route takes her past the Fish Market. Opposite is the old Subscription Library where Stoker discovered the name Dracula. Go along St Ann's Staith to the bridge.

Cross harbour by the bridge (referred to as the Drawbridge in the book). The old, wooden lifting bridge was demolished in 1835 by the Victorians and replaced with an iron swing-bridge. Mina has to run across it to the east side in order to reach the churchyard.

Turn left at the top of Bridge Street into **Church Street**, looking very much as it did at the period of *Dracula*, with quaint yards and passages leading off between houses and down to the water's edge. Mina has to run the length of the dark silent street, past the old Town Hall to the cluster of houses below the cliff known as **Tate Hill**.

Fork left to Tate Hill, down the steps on the left, onto the long stone jetty which projects onto the lower harbour, flanked by the sands. It is here, on the night of a mysterious and sudden storm, that the Russian schooner *Demeter* (chartered by Dracula) is driven through the harbour entrance and crashes ashore. (Based on a real-life incident in 1885 and photographed by Sutcliffe.) The Captain is

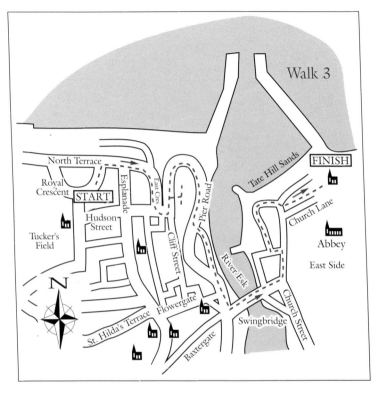

found dead, the crew missing, the only life aboard an immense black dog which leaps from the ship, runs along the pier helter-skelter up the 199 Church Stairs to go and hide in the graveyard.

Follow the path round to where Church Street joins Henrietta Street at the foot of the **Church Stairs**. There are 199 of these stone steps, and in her frantic dash to rescue Lucy, Mina races up every one of them. Alongside the stairs is the stepped road known as **Church Lane**. Mina also mentions this in her diary under its old nickname The Donkey Road.

At the top of the Church Stairs is the picturesque parish church of St Mary's. Looking beyond the tower you can glimpse a section of the cliffside path and graveyard – though not very far because of a dip in the ground. It is from this point that Mina catches sight of Lucy, apparently asleep on their favourite seat – though not alone; there is something long and black bending over her. Mina's view is lost as she continues to run up the path. By the time she reaches the seat Lucy is alone.

Continue up the path, then turn left, until you pass the corner of the church tower. Somewhere here, just off the path in front of the long Gothic windows, must have been the girls' favourite seat, sheltered from the west winds and looking out across the harbour to their lodgings in 'the Crescent'.

There is no trace of the flat topped thruff-steean (tombstone) belonging to one George Cannon – a suicide, buried as an accidental death! But countless graves have disintegrated with weathering and been lost through subsidence over the years.

The favourite seat does not feel quite the same to Mina after the night on which she finds Lucy there and escorts her home. Even less so when she recalls the death of their friend, the old sailor Mr Swales, whose body had been found with its neck broken on that very seat earlier in the day.

It later transpires that Count Dracula, as well as assuming the shape of a big black dog and a bat has, when in human form, taken refuge for part of his stay in Whitby in the unhallowed grave of a suicide.

As for the timber and wrought iron seat, it probably was very similar to the one on the West Cliff dedicated to the memory of the man who created one of the world's great immortal characters and in so doing helped to immortalise the town of Whitby.

To complete the Gothic melodrama, why not do as Stoker did and gravitate towards the imposing ruins of the Abbey which, as he was to note in *Dracula,* is mentioned in Walter Scott's poem *Marmion* and has a legend of a ghostly white lady – a role unwittingly imitated by Lucy in the novel.

East side

Monks and authors

2 miles in length and takes about 1¹/₂ hours.
Start and finish on the east side of the swing bridge

From where Bridge Street connects with Church Street enter Green's Yard and climb the steps. On the left is the Donkey Field. Follow the old Monks' trod on the left which leads to **Abbey Plain**. Enjoy the fine views over the town and out to sea. The last building on the right, now the YHA, was a former stable block for the Abbey. To the right of the Abbey gatehouse and along the drive stands **Abbey House** – rebuilt by the Cholmleys after the Dissolution of the Monasteries in the mid-16th century and redesigned during the reign of Charles II. The part seen from the access drive is a late 17th century hall of impressive proportions. It was ruined in a great storm in 1775 and never rebuilt. During the Civil War the house was held for the King, but was seized by the inhabitants of Whitby for Lord Fairfax. During the period 1670- 1730 a huge 'stone' garden was built to front the hall. Unlike any other in the world, it is being restored by English Heritage to its former glory under the Whitby Headland Project and will provide an interpretation and visitors' centre for life on the headland from Saxon times.

On the Abbey Plain or hereabouts stood the original Celtic Abbey founded by Oswy, King of Northumbria. In AD664 the Abbess Hilda presided over the great Synod of Whitby which sought to unite the Celtic and Catholic Churches in Western Europe and settle the date for Easter. Danish Vikings destroyed the abbey in AD867.

The Abbey was re-established for the Benedictine Order, in the 11th century, by Reinfrid under the patronage of William de Percy. At the height of importance it was one of the richest houses in Yorkshire and controlled extensive lands. The bulk of the buildings still standing date from the 12th and 13th centuries.

The Parish Church of **St Mary's** originates about AD1110 and was sponsored by the Abbott for use by the town and the manorial tenants. Its unusual galleries date from between 1695-1835. The three-decker pulpit of 1778 enables the preacher to 'rake' every part of the church. Behind it, supported on barleycorn twist columns, is the Cholmley pew, access to which is gained by an outside staircase! Underneath that staircase is the unique Huntstrodd Memorial.

Caedmon's Cross

Caedmon's Cross, situated at the top of the 199 stairs, was erected in 1898 to Commemorate Caedmon, the first English poet who was a 'landsman' in the Anglo Saxon Monastery. The Cross is carved from Northumbrian sandstone in the Celtic design with the figures of Christ, David, Abbess Hilda and Caedmon in panels.

The 199 **Church Stairs** were first referred to in 1370 and were wooden. In 1774 they were changed into stone. The flat sections or landings were designed for 'easement of the bearers of coffins' as folk were 'lifted' up the stairs.

The stone track adjacent to the Church Stairs leads from Church Street to Abbey House and is known as **The Donkey Road**. Originally it led to the great east door of the abbey and was used for processional purposes on feast and high days. Its top section was re-routed in the 1860s when a new boundary wall was built over part of the 'stone' garden.

21

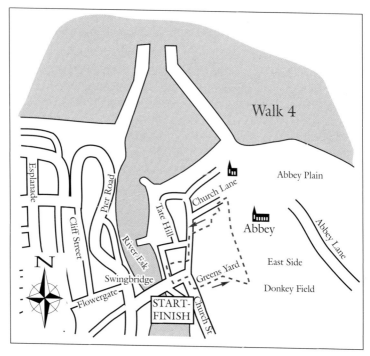

Start descending the Donkey Road and at the first house on the left turn into Abbey Terrace East. At the end go down several flights of steps which brings you into **Blackburn's Yard**. Note the plaque of the site of the birthplace of Whitby's Victorian novelist Mary Linskill (1840-91) whose work was much admired by Gladstone. Mary's father was the local constable and he kept a 'Hoppit' or Lockup at the bottom of the yard, near the public washhouse (now a pottery).

The penultimate building on the left, a three-storeyed terrace cottage in this the heart of the oldest part of town, is typical of a fisherman's home. It had been adapted over the centuries but retains 17th and 18th century features including mullioned windows.

Turn left into **Church Street**. On the corner of the market place is the Walrus and Carpenter, the name celebrating the author Lewis Carroll's visits to the town. However, the building has above the door

22

lintel a stone inscribed HGE 1764; it was formerly an inn named House of the Black Bull.

The **market place** AD1640 supplanted the older market place at the foot of Golden Lion Bank on the west side. The so-called Town Hall was built in 1788 in the classical style by Jonathon Pickernell, Harbour Engineer and builder of the West Pier, for Mr. Nathaniel Cholmley, the Lord of the Manor. The Town Hall or Tollbooth as it is sometimes called is adorned by the armorial bearings of the Cholmley family, whose connection with Whitby dates back to the Dissolution of the Abbey.

The weathervane atop the clock tower recalls the golden days of the fishing industry. The market place was also where the public whipping of thieves and beggars took place and where the stocks resided.

In the mid-18th century Whitby boasted of being the seventh largest port in England, based on the tonnage of shipping using its harbour facilities. Those ships need victualling and the area around the Market Square contained many butchers' shops. The Artist's Studio on the right was once a butcher's shop and slaughterhouse. Chains and hooks from that grisly occupation still festoon the ceiling.

23

The **Market Hall**, part of which is now a public convenience, was built as a covered market, fruit and vegetables being sold upstairs, with the shambles underneath. Milk, butter, cheese, eggs and poultry were sold under the colonnades of the Town Hall. Facing the market place in Church Street is the Black Horse public house, in whose yard a midden from Whitby's first Abbey was found. It contained a seal from Rome dating back to AD679.

Further along Church Street is the **White Horse and Griffin**. Erected in 1681, the house has many associations with the past life of the town, having been the meeting place for master mariners and local gentry who met for both business and pleasure. It is mentioned by Whitby author Ethel Kidson in her novel *Herringfleet* and Charles Dickens recorded that oyster-shell grottoes were a feature when he stayed. From this inn the stagecoaches departed to York in the 1760s following the opening of the turnpike road, the fifty mile journey taking two days. The first diligence to run from Whitby to York in 1788 made its headquarters here and in later years it became the centre for the horse-drawn carrying trade.

Opposite the White Horse and Griffin, take a narrow passage on your right, into Ellerby Lane. Originally it led onto the stepping stones across the Harbour to St Anne's Lane. Different stonework between the houses in Sandgate shows where the lane became Fish Ghaut for its last few yards onto the stepping stones. It was bricked up following the fire of 1866, when the then candlemaking factory caught fire and buildings as far as the bridge to the left were burnt down.

From Sandgate take a right turn and before you is the swing bridge.

Four piers

2 miles in length and takes about 1½ hours.
Start and finish from the west side of the swing bridge

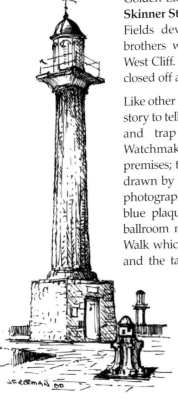

The lighthouse

From the west side of the swing bridge, go up Golden Lion Bank and take the third right into **Skinner Street**. This formed part of the Farndale Fields development in 1762 by the Skinner brothers which began the colonisation of the West Cliff. Originally the street was a cul-de-sac, closed off at its northern end by a ropewalk.

Like other streets in Whitby, every building has a story to tell. The Doctor's residence with its pony and trap ready for an urgent call; the Watchmaker with a large clock outside his premises; the Undertaker with his ornate hearse drawn by plumed horses; the original studio of photographer Frank Sutcliffe, denoted by the blue plaque on the antique shop; the former ballroom now the Evangelical Church; Routh Walk which housed Dr John Routh's Academy; and the tall building at the head of the walk, Tower Flats, an attempt to improve the working conditions of the jet workers back in 1880.

Further up the street, flanked by a row of steps, is Harold Private Hotel, now shops and flats. Behind these is Tanshelf, a perfect embodiment of a Georgian town house. On the right is Bothams Bakery, started in the

25

1860s by Mrs Elizabeth Botham when she was landlady of the Hole in the Wall Pub. On the other side of the road stands the Granby Hotel. Take the cobbled side street to its right, which leads to what was once West Cliff farm, with its row of cottages for the farm labourers. Exit right into John Street via the arch, turning left and crossing the street into Crescent Avenue. The Church of St Hilda's is on your left. Take a right into Hudson Street and head east towards the **Khyber Pass,** with its views across the harbour and the east cliff.

The house at the top of the Khyber Pass, 'Streonshalh', looks two storeyed, but is deceptive, having several storeys to its rear which go down the cliff side. The building at the end of Cliff Street with a bell atop was formerly Mount School.

Advancing along **East Terrace,** towards the sea, you come to the Whale Bone Arch. Descend the steps and cross the road emerging at the Lifeboat Museum, with its proud history and memorabilia. The lifeboats were launched down the slipway to the left, above which is Battery Parade so called from the gun battery which once stood there with its eight guns and roundhouse magazine stores. The area containing the bandstand is known as Scotch Head.

The **West Pier** is first mentioned in the reign of Henry VIII, who ordered its maintenance with timber from the 'Kings Wood'; it was rebuilt in 1632 with stone in a timber frame. In 1702, an act of parliament decreed that to assist with its maintenance, a duty of 6d per caldron of coal carried, should be paid on coastal shipping carrying coal. The head of the pier contained a further six gun battery, which was dismantled after the Napoleonic Wars.

In 1831, within the short space of eleven weeks, a handsome lighthouse, some eighty feet high, in the form of a Greek Doric column was erected, complete with an octagonal lantern.

The extensions, made of concrete and timber complete with decking, much reduces the swell in the harbour, and were completed in 1912. They form a delightful promenade and a 'pier-ender' is a fine appetiser before a meal.

On returning to Scotch Head, note the 19th century furniture such as capstans and mooring posts by which ships were warped into harbour or tied up.

Going upstream on **Pier Road**, amusement arcades occupy the landward side. The tall structure on the riverside is for making and discharging ice to the fishing boats.

At the fish quay, fish is landed from boats, sorted and auctioned. The large building opposite, now a fish restaurant, was in 1826 the Whitby Subscription Library, Museum and Public Slipper Baths. Keep to the riverside onto Marine Parade.

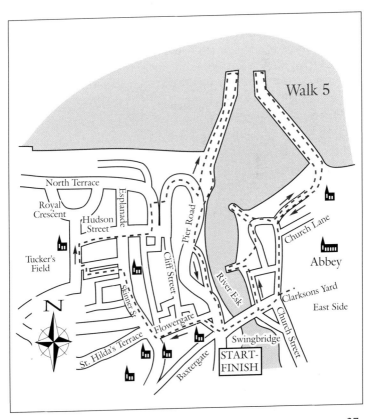

The Dracula Experience – for many years a photographer's studio – was built in 1813 as Whitby Commercial Newsroom. It originally fronted on to Haggersgate, but with the new construction of the quay it acquired a new frontage.

Crossing the swing bridge turn first left into **Sandgate**. Now full of curio collectors, it used to be better known as Low Butchergate. The penultimate shop on your left still displays a tiled frontage depicting its former wares.

In the market square on your left is the former **Market Hall**. Meat was sold downstairs, fruit and vegetables upstairs. Milk, butter, cheese, eggs and chickens retailed from the steps under the Town Hall. At the end of the Market Hall, you approach the Fish Pier. Here fish was landed and sold in the market place during the 18th century. When the fish market was moved to the west side, the pier became known as the liteboat pier; adjacent to it are the lifeboat house and berth for the lifeboat which is always on station.

Exit down the slipway, up the steps to your right, into New Way Ghaut, then left into Church Street. The house on the corner now used as a headquarters by a rowing club was the Lady Cholmley Day School.

Where Church Street turns right, a path in front of the public house leads onto Tate Pier; known as the **Burgess Pier**, it was enlarged in 1766. In 1841 it was used in connection with the herring industry and there was a boiler house and large herring house close by. It later played host to the Whitby lifeboat. One launch, in particular, brought hardship and grief to many in the town when on 3rd of February 1861, eleven members of the 12-man crew lost their lives. The survivor, Henry Freeman, was trying out a new fangled buoyancy aid – a cork waistcoat.

The sandy area next to the pier, **Tate Hill Sands**, is also known as Colliers Hope and was used as a sheltering place in inclement weather for the coal ships sailing from Newcastle to London.

At the foot of the 199 Church Stairs is **Henrietta Street**. At its end, kippers are still cured in the traditional way in the smoke house.

Beyond, the street reverts to its original name of Haggerlyth, where another battery of guns was housed.

The **East Pier**, circa 1702, does not actually connect with the land, other than by an elevated walkway, the 'spaw ladder'. Extended in a north-west direction in 1844-50, one can still make out the original half round end embedded in the later masonry. The lighthouse at the end was erected in 1854.

Returning to Church Street, a house at the bottom of the **Church Stairs** has ammonites embedded in the wall and a nearby dwelling has inscribed "Leonard and Isabel Hart built in the year of our Lord 1705." Further down Church Street is the now defunct Wesley Chapel next to which is a flight of stairs which lead to the Old Methodist Chapel built in 1788 and opened by John Wesley.

The Georgian period saw the development of the numerous 'yards', for as the town expanded, landowners built cottages and tenement blocks to the rear of their properties. This led to overcrowding, but leaves us with a legacy of 188 buildings listed as of national and architectural interest in Church Street and its yards. One such on the right is **Arguments Yard**, named after Thomas Argument who built a cottage in Church Street with its back garden running down to the riverside. Later he erected in that garden five cottages which were then rented out to families.

Before leaving Church Street, past the White Horse and Griffin, take a narrow passage on your left into Clarksons Yard. This Whitby gem features highly in the annual Britain in Bloom contest, largely because the cottages on the right side have been demolished, giving it an open south facing aspect and a climate more akin to the Mediterranean.

Depart the yard by turning left and you are in **Bridge Street**. Turn to the right and before you is the swing bridge.

Seaside saunter

2½ miles in length and takes about two hours.
Start and finish at the Royal Hotel, West Cliff

High on the **West Cliff,** the Victorian architecture of the Royal Hotel
dominates the sands and harbour of Whitby, and it is from here that
we commence our promenade by the sea.

Putting the Whalebones and Captain Cook's Monument on your
right, walk down the drive that leads to the **Pavilion Complex.**
Nestling into the cliff it gives wonderful views out over the North Sea,
the piers and a glorious stretch of beach along to Sandsend.

Spanning time with a Victorian theatre and a recently-built Northern
Lights suite, the Pavilion Complex results in a multi-functional venue

suitable for almost every type of event. The traditional proscenium arch theatre, originally called the Westcliff Saloon, was built in1878 by Sir George Elliott for his wife, a former Gaiety girl. It soon became the centre of 'variety' and the arts for miles around. The gargoyles outside the building are said to depict famous actors of the day. Purchased in 1915 by the local authority, the policy of providing all-round family entertainment has continued over the years.

Go down under the archway and below the Crystal Lounge and Northern Lights suite. The original glass Floral Pavilion, built in the 1920s, was demolished in 1989 and rebuilt into the multi-purpose modern building. Its large porthole windows boast magnificent views over the sea and three weeks either side of the summer solstice you can see the sun rise and set in the sea. Situated beneath the Northern Lights suite is the Exhibition Hall or Undercroft, with its large windows, which look out to sea.

Head along the new sea wall, with views out to sea on the right. On the left is the exit of the cliff lift; further along is a plaque on the wall which declares that Sir Leon Brittain opened the new sea defences in 1988. Next are the wooden steps leading up to Happy Valley and finally with the curve of the wall enter **Upgang Ravine**.

Here a stream rushes to the sea and a slipway recalls the days when it was a lifeboat launching station. Atop the cliff, in the 18th century, stood the Mulgrave Arms, a renowned haunt of smugglers. The sea claimed the ancient inn and the cliff top and the 19th century railway line has given way to an 18-hole golf course.

Go up the ravine and take the last path on the left, before the golfers' footbridge spanning the ravine. Then follows a pleasant cliff-top saunter. The house with a red roofed tower over an arch with a low white wall and open space beyond housed the 'Spider's Web' outdoor swimming pool till the early 1990s. It still lies buried beneath the grassed area. The large green roofed house by the top of the wooden steps, with stained glass windows, was a former miners' welfare home. Upon reaching the main road Moorlands is to your right. This Methodist Guild Holiday Hotel was the home of a former sea captain, with bedrooms built to resemble ships' cabins.

Further along the cliff top, the large four-towered **Metropole Hotel** is the only steel framed building in the town. The towers move when buffeted by the strong north-eastern winter gales. The establishment boasted electric lights at a time when many private homes were just installing 'modern' gas lighting. During the first world war German battleships used its high profile silhouette as target practice, and a memorial mound nearby recalls a young soldier's death as a result of a bombardment.

At the bottom of Argyle Road on the other side of the roundabout is **Station Avenue** and the site of the West Cliff railway station where people arrived by rail for a fortnight or month-long holiday. Complete with maids and luggage, they were transported to their summer residence by horse drawn cab. The rail line to the 'Top Town' station is closed. The buildings remain, but are now a builder's yard.

From North Promenade, cliff paths known locally as the zigzags can be walked down to reach the beach. The cliff lift only dates from 1930.

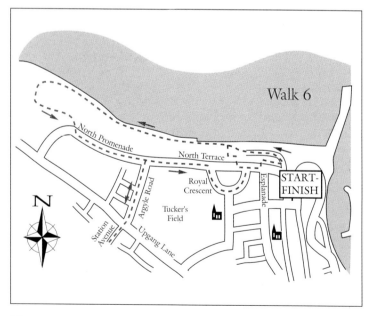

Along from the West Cliff amusements of mini-golf, boating, go-karting and paddling pool are the **Royal Crescent Gardens**.

Towards the end of 1843, plans by Mr G. Matthew of Whitby for a large terrace development on the West Cliff were made public and a company presided over by George Hudson the 'Railway King' was formed. By 1846, with Hudson, the chair, Whitby Cliff Building Company were entering into contracts for the making of bricks. Hudson, upon becoming a Member of Parliament, pressed ahead with improvements to Whitby, which was clearly his favourite holiday resort. Thus was born a handsome range of residences extending from the Union Mill (now Harrison's Garage) at the inland extremity to terraces of town houses upon West Cliff, on the seaward promontory.

The centrepiece was Royal Crescent overlooking the Crescent Gardens designed by the Newcastle Architect John Dobson. Numbers 1-16 were completed forming half a crescent. The other segment, locally known as Hudson's Palace, was to be a 200-bed apartment block for the Railway King to enjoy holidays in Whitby. Hudson, having purchased the Pickering to Whitby line, and converted it from a horse drawn railway into steam in 1847, no doubt hoped to make a lot of money with the development of what became known as Whitby New Town.

The development was seen as a noble scheme to secure a position of prosperity for the future welfare of the town. By 1859 the money had run out, Hudson had lost his seat in Parliament and had to flee to the continent to escape the bailiffs of the North Eastern Railways to whom he owed share dealings in excess of £160,000. The 'New Town' project was never completed and Royal Crescent was left undeveloped. The building on the other side of the car park entrance was to be in 1939 Whitby's newest hotel, The Princess Alexandra. The outbreak of World War Two disrupted the opening and it became a nursing and convalescent home.

Across from Crescent Gardens is the upper entrance to the Pavilion Complex. In the foyer are some wonderful embroidered panels, loaned by the Friends of Whitby Abbey, the work having been done by the women of Whitby and District to commemorate the 450th anniversary of the dissolution of Whitby Abbey.

The Spa booking office is all that is left of the entrance into the formal Spa gardens. The drive down to the West Cliff Saloon now doubles as car parking as it returns us to our starting place overlooking the harbour and the sands.

West side

Ancient and modern

2 miles in length and takes about 1½ hours.
Start and finish at the swing bridge

From the west side of the swing bridge, go left along St Ann's Staith, where houses once jutted into the harbour, and follow the road round into **Haggersgate** or Hacklesougate AD1296.

The Whitby Mission on your left was built for John Yeoman in 1760; it became the Mission to seamen in 1877. The recreation room, beyond the main house, completed in 1963, contains a mural depicting the east side of Whitby by H. Lambert Smith, which occupies the whole of the west wall.

After the Star Inn, a typical Georgian building having a bay over an arch, go through and up the steps of **Bakehouse Yard**. At the top a plaque on the wall is dedicated to lifeboatman Henry Freeman. In Cliff Street turn left to observe a fine dwelling built in 1888 to a Dutch design, which has ammonite fossils set in the wall panels and unique window patterns.

Climb the stairs to **The Paddock**. The Auction Rooms used to be the Whitby Theatre between 1763 and 1784. In nearby Silver Street, turn right, and advance beyond the salerooms and Bothams Bakery to where it becomes Wellington Terrace and carry on to Crescent Place; turning right, cross the road and enter East Terrace. Halfway along descend the steps and cross the Khyber Pass to enter a tunnel, which frames a classic view of the abbey.

Exit from the tunnel by descending the steps onto **the Cragg;** this was once one of the rookeries leading to many small yards tucked under the foot of the cliff. At the bottom turn right along the pathway between the cottages. Take the cobbled Pier Lane, which returns you to **Cliff Street** via a slanting walkway. Originally the lane led to the Cliffs and had a wicket gate at the end to prevent cattle entering the town. Going left along Cliff Street, observe some of the 19 properties on the national list of buildings of Architectural or Historic Interest. Beyond The Paddock, on the left, a small public garden is opposite a former bakehouse built in 1691.

Enter Macklins Yard across a small private car park and take an obvious passage into Flowergate and turn right. Cross Flowergate and take a left down Brunswick Street; on the left are some historic cottages.

Take the first narrow road on your right – the houses on the left in Brunswick Terrace were built on the site of the Whitby Theatre, burnt down in 1806. The lane leads to Union Steps, used to transport corn to the Union Mill. Descend these steps crossing Walker Street and process to Bagdale with its shipowners' mansions.

In Bagdale turn right. The raised footpath forms part of the old Monks' causeway leading to Skelder top and over the moors to Guisborough. Under the road flows Bagdale Beck, AD1391, which was enclosed in 1866. Opposite Broomfield Terrace, where at no 9 the De Maurier family often visited, is **Pannett Park**.

Opened in 1928, its ten acres are a testament to the foresight of North Riding County Alderman R. E. Pannett who purchased the former market gardens in 1901, and bequeathed the land into 'gardens of rest for Whitby'.

He also provided an art gallery which, in addition to providing facilities for local artists' exhibitions, has within its rooms a number of paintings by George Weatherill, a talented Whitby artist whose work is much sought after.

Attached to the gallery is the museum. Founded in 1823 and independently owned by the Literary and Philosophical Society, it contains a fascinating collection of artefacts including world renowned fossils. The Shipping wing has models made from animal

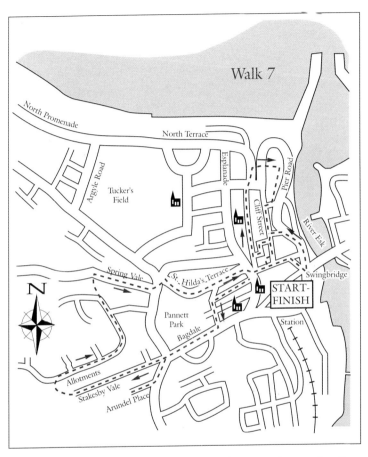

bones and human hair by Napoleonic prisoners of war. Another wing houses Captain Cook memorabilia with models of ships and equipment used by the whaling industry and Captain Scoresby.

At the junction with Bagdale and Chubb Hill cross the road into **Southend Gardens**. To the left is Arundel House Hotel, erected in 1820 for banker Robert Campion. To the rear is a terrace of cottages with coach house and stables.

The tunnel on the right of the main house, through the railway embankment which carried the line from West Cliff station to Whitby, leads into Stakesby Vale. The disused line is currently a public footpath which leads to the thirteen-arched viaduct which spans the river Esk.

To the left, through the tunnel, the furniture warehouse is a converted sail-making loft and ropery dating from the 1700s. Upon reaching the gate take the stepped pathway on the right into Kirkham Road. The modern corner house has a plaque recalling when German battleships shelled Whitby.

Keeping the allotments on your right and modern bungalows on the left, Byland Road is reached. The large building on the right is a converted convent which now houses the Functional English Christian Language Centre.

Crossing Rievaulx Road the grassed area is bisected by a stone pathway. Follow it between the Medical Centre buildings to emerge in Stakesby Road and turn right towards the roundabout.

Cross Chubb Hill Road into **St Hilda's Terrace**. Behind, at the top of the hill on the site of Harrison's garage, stood the Union Windmill; to your right an entrance to Pannett Park; ahead St Hilda's Terrace – Whitby's premier Georgian terrace, begun in 1778. Known as the New Buildings when erected on open fields above Flowergate, the houses vary greatly in size, the smallest being at the western end. A service road running behind contains a number of coach houses.

At the junction of Skinner Street, is Church House, now a centre for community activities, and next door Trinity (United Reform) Church. Opposite, **Flowergate House** probably dates from 1761, designed by John Addison for Thomas Campion, Gentleman and Shipowner. It was converted into the Crown Hotel in 1868 to cater for "the large proportion of the highest and most fashionable ranks of society" who arrived in Whitby by the new fangled contraption: the railway. In 1870 it hosted a meeting to promote the idea of a railway between Whitby and Scarborough. The elegant frontage and twin entrance staircase are now masked by shops, built in what was the front garden to the mansion.

Flowergate, mentioned in the Domesday Book as the Manor of Flore, is now a shopping street of 18th and 19th century buildings, the upper storeys retaining much of their original appearances. At the junction with Brunswick Street is the Little Angel Inn, a very ancient property and reputed to be Florum Castle built in the reign of King Stephen (1135-1154). Windows to the back of the property date back to Charles I. Outside Ye Olde Abbey Inn is a mounting block for horse riders.

Waterloo Place on the left displays some modern dwellings built on the site of a former cinema, covered market hall and jet factory.

Moving down Flowergate, a solicitor's office on the left was constructed on the site of a 17th century Court House, the House of Correction and Gaolers Lodging, instituted in 1636. The underground gaol cells are boarded over under the main window. On the opposite side of the road the Rose and Crown Yard had a slaughterhouse behind the then street-fronted butcher's shop and cows were driven down the narrow alley. A stone above a doorway is inscribed Thomas & Elizabeth Walker 1705.

German bombs demolished part of Flowergate in 1941; the area now contains a supermarket. **The Sutcliffe Gallery** on the corner of Golden Lion Bank is dedicated to the work of the world-famous Victorian photographer whose camera captured so much of the atmosphere of old Whitby.

Exit down Golden Lion Bank to return to the swing bridge.

Walk Eight

Three bridges and a ford

2¹/₂ miles in length and takes about two hours.
Start and finish west side of the swing bridge

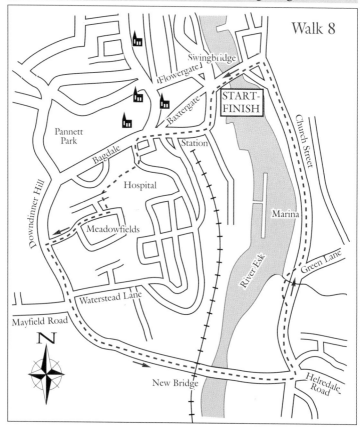

Whitby's development has been formed by the River Esk and the estuary has for centuries provided a haven for shipping on this long and formidable coastline. The river has its source on the moors high above Westerdale, some twenty-three miles up the Esk Valley.

Within the surrounding area were a number of mills and ironstone workings together with religious houses and monastic granges. Much travelling would have been done between these houses and workplaces with packhorses carrying fleeces, fish and other products of industry, so the need for good river crossings was important. In medieval times, providing money in one's will for the maintenance of roads and bridges was a pious act, designed, perhaps, to guarantee one a place in heaven.

Whitby now boasts two bridges, the lower swing bridge and the high level bridge of recent addition. The first bridge, which no doubt put the ferry boat out of business, was first mentioned in 1351 during the reign of Edward III, when pontage (the collection of tolls) was granted for its repair, charges being made per horse or cartload.

By 1610 sixty oaks were needed for rebuilding and thirty years later more money was required as mariners were damaging the bridge by tying their ships to it. Large ships were being built in the 1700s and the bridge required widening to accommodate them. During 1766-67 a drawbridge was constructed on stone piers. On March 27th 1835 a new swivel bridge was opened at a cost of £2,600. A wider electrically-driven swivel bridge replaced this in 1909.

Leaving the old bridge follow **New Quay Road** with its fine views looking up river. The shape of road and dock result from reclaimed works undertaken in Victorian times. Formerly it was Belle Island where the wooden sail ships unloaded their ballast cargo. Endeavour Wharf is used to unload cargoes of steel and timber from the Baltic and Continental ports.

Turn left at **Bagdale Hall**, that fine Tudor building with a pelican on the gable end of the roof. Up Spring Hill on the left are Princes Cottages, across the road, Bagdale Travel Lodge, once known as Lobster Hall because it was built by the guard of the Whitby-York stagecoach from the profits of carrying lobsters. At its gatepost follow the flagged path by the side of the hospital into the Meadowfield housing estate, turning right to emerge part way up Prospect Hill, the new road into Whitby back in the late 1800s.

Turning left cross Waterstead Lane (by the traffic lights). The gatepost and drive on your left lead to St Colombus, built by Admiral Moorsom of Trafalgar fame. Stay on the main road which continues onto the new high level bridge, erected in 1979 to remedy the traffic congestion which occurred at the swing bridge. The then Marquis of Normanby performed the opening ceremony on 21st March 1980.

Looking down river, almost under the shelter of the bridge on the right hand bank, is the one-time shipyard of Messrs T. Turnbull and Son. They began the building of iron steamships in 1871, launching 116 vessels of 800-6,000 tons between that date and 1902 when the yard closed down. On the left hand bank, the old quay has an arch in it, now bricked up, which was an overflow from the Roman style bathhouse which Admiral Moorsom had built in the basement of his hilltop hall of residence.

Leaving the bridge with a left hand turn, opposite Larpool, is **Gallows Close**, scene of many a grisly hanging in the days when the Abbots had the power of life, death and banishment for miscreants against the laws of the land.

A little further on is the entrance to Whitehall shipyard. California Beck is crossed by Spital Bridge, so called from a leper hospital founded here by the first Abbot of Whitby in AD1109. In the 1700s the tributary to the Esk was dammed up and used as a timber pond to keep the shipbuilding material in condition.

The road to the right is **Green Lane**, or the Hearse Road, because it was used by funerals going to the Parish Church, though many old Whitby folk preferred to be carried up the Church Stairs.

Near Spital Bridge, on the banks of the Esk, a paved road can be noticed, this being part of the ancient **Bog Hall** ford which crossed the river at this point. It is thought to be the original crossing, long anterior to any bridges nearer the sea.

Further on is **Boyes' Staith** or **Abraham's Bosom**. It is here that on the eve of Ascension Day each year the Horngarth is now planted, with the ancient ritual of horn blowing and crying of "out on Ye" by the seneschal of the Lord of the Manor. The ceremony of building a hedge of latticed branches dates back almost 900 years. Its origins are disputed – either it was a fence, in which some of the Abbot's goods were stored and it required annual maintenance by his tenants, or as in the more popular belief, it was all to do with a boar hunt in which a hermit monk was killed by nobles, for which the planting of a hedge was their penance.

Abraham's Bosom was extensively used in the days of sailing ships for careening. The sides and bottom of the ships would be scraped and cleaned of foulness caused by long voyages without risk of damage to their hulls whilst lying on the sand.

The rose gardens belong to the Seamen Hospital and the nearby Fleece Inn gained a street front access when it was rebuilt following the demolition and widening of Church Street in the late 1950-early 1960s. Car parks have replaced dwelling houses, warehouses and Church of St Michael.

Badgale Hall

The slipway, adjacent to the car park, formed part of that old alley-way called **Tin Ghaut**. (A ghaut is an alleyway which runs from the street onto the riverside.) It was one of the landing places for ships moored above the bridge and was used when the upper harbour was crowded with shipping, for taking refuge from the winter gales and the turbulent North Sea raging outside the harbour bar.

Crossing Grape Lane, continue past the three-tiered Merchants House on the corner into Bridge Street and ahead of you is the swing bridge.

43

Christian heritage and churches

2 miles in length and takes about 1¹/₂ hours.
Start at the Abbey Plain, finish Haggersgate

With over a thousand years of ecclesiastical history to its credit one cannot ignore the Christian heritage of Whitby from its earliest beginnings in AD658 when Oswy King of Northumbria, wanting to consolidate his Christian Kingdom, twixt the Rivers Humber and the Tweed, took battle with Penda the Pagan King of Mercia.

Oswy vowed that if God would grant him victory, he would give twelve parcels of land for the development of abbeys and monasteries. Moreover he would devote his daughter Aelfeda to the Lord to be a holy virgin.

With the battle of Winwidfield duly won by Oswy's forces and in fulfilment of his vow, land was given for the founding of the Monastery of Streonshalh. Lady Hilda, the King's niece, in holy orders at Hartlepool, was appointed the first Abbess. In 664 the Abbess Hilda presided over the great Synod of Whitby which settled the date of Easter and united the Celtic and Roman Churches. The Abbey and the town of the same name was destroyed by the Danes in AD867 and lay desolate for close on two hundred years, the memory of St Hilda continuing among the ruins.

It was revived in 1078 by Reinfrid, a former soldier in the Norman Conqueror's army, who sought leave of the King to build an Abbey on the sacred site. With the arrival of the Benedictine Monks the town of Whitby began to grow. Its growing wealth and prosperity attracted the attention of King Harold of Norway who in 1127 led a raiding

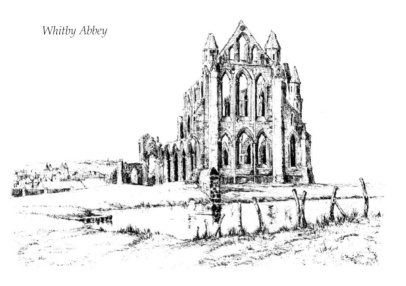

Whitby Abbey

party and sacked the second Abbey and the township. Some 30 years later, rebuilding started on a much enhanced scheme which was to house at the peak of its fame some forty monks.

King Henry VIII's Dissolution of Monasteries Act saw the Abbot surrender the abbey to the Crown, and the abbey and its lands were sold off to the highest bidder. The stark ruins and remains of the third abbey, seen today, date from the 12th and 13th centuries.

St Mary's Parish Church was built around AD 1110, probably on the site of a church dating back to Saxon times. The stone-flagged pathway leading from the abbey into the church are the covers of vaults. Most of the charm of the building springs from its original interior; the exterior gives virtually no indication of what is inside apart from the Georgian windows and external steps to the multitude of galleries.

Depart the church and descend the 199 church stairs, and pause on the last landing. From here John Wesley the renegade Anglican priest preached nonconformity. The Methodists built an octagonal chapel at

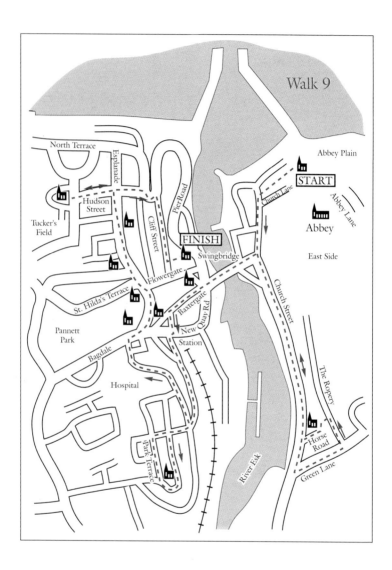

the end of Haggerlyth which fell into the sea following a landslip. It was replaced in 1788 in Church Street, the approach being up some steps to the right of Wesley Hall.

Further down Church Street at the corner of the market place, the Monks Haven was reputed to be a chapel of ease prior to the reformation.

Continuing down Church Street, on the left is the Primitive Methodists' Chapel, now converted into a private dwelling named **Ammonite House**. The steps leading to the entrance have been cut away to allow car access into the building. Above the door the carved heads are thought to be of John and Charles Wesley. A nearby yard is still referred to as Ranters' Meeting Yard.

Opposite (now a car park) stood the Anglican **Church of St Michael** whilst further up Church Street the Catholic **Church of St Peter** is small and unpretentious. Turn left up Green Lane; the houses on the left are built on the site of the workhouse mortuary. First left, part of the old Union Workhouse now hosts **Kingdom Hall**, the meeting place for Jehovah 's Witnesses.

Exit from the Ropery after crossing the road leading into the car park, down a narrow footpath on your left called Salt Pan Well Steps. At the bottom turn right along Church Street heading into town. Just past Grape Lane, on the left, is the **Friends' Meeting House**, a rebuilding in 1813 of an earlier establishment of 1676.

Cross the bridge and in front of the HSBC Bank, in 1595 was a "howse called a chappell" believed to be where the monks on bridge toll duty resided, pre-Reformation.

In Baxtergate is **St Ninian's**. A proprietary church (owned by the thirty original share owners and their successors), it was built in 1778 to supplement the Parish Church for the growing population on the west side of the town. Dedicated to one of the early Celtic saints, it is thought to have replaced a medieval chapel on another site.

Leaving Baxtergate by Wellington Road, cross over and go along Windsor Terrace. Go up North Road and second left into Park Terrace. At the far end, in Park Place, is **Fishburn Park Methodist Chapel**, built to serve the inhabitants of "Railway City " as the new late Victorian houses of Fishburn Park estate were known. It is currently undergoing a revival as Fishburn Park Christian Centre under the New Life Church banner.

Retrace your steps to Victoria Square and at the junction of Brunswick Street and Baxtergate is the Anglican **Church of St John**. The 19th Century saw the provision and redevelopment and enlargement of many churches in Whitby. The Catholic Church of St Hilda, on the opposite corner, built in 1867, is an example, replacing a more modest structure of 1805. Up the hill the present Brunswick Chapel dates from 1891. Its predecessor was built in what was then Skate Lane in 1814.

At the top of Brunswick Street is Flowergate. To the right is the old **Unitarian Chapel** established in 1695; the current building dates from 1715. To the left is the **United Reform Church**. Its exterior remains placid but internally it has been radically altered to serve the local community in a variety of different ways as the Trinity Centre.

Up Skinner Street and on the left the **Evangelical Church** has kept the external facade of the old ballroom, but altered the inside dramatically. At the top of Skinner Street, the **Congregational Church** is another Victorian edifice struggling to make ends meet with an ageing, dwindling congregation.

Left and at the top of Hudson Street/Abbey Terrace is The Anglican **Church of St Hilda's**. It was intended to serve the needs of the growing middle-class population of the West Cliff. This large imposing building was designed by R. J. Johnson of Newcastle. Opened in 1889 it contains some interesting stained glass windows.

From Abbey Terrace, cross into Crescent Place, follow the road to the right, into the wide sweep of East Crescent. At the Old Mount School, now a dance centre, turn right into Cliff Street. Cut across the car park on the left and down the steps to reach Paradise Yard and the riverside in Haggersgate. The former Yeoman Mansion has been converted into **The Mission**. The chapel upstairs, utilised by the Methodists, is worthy of a visit and is in keeping with the former occupants of this Georgian town house.